IC/GM&O

Color Guide to Freight and Passenger Equipment

James Kinkaid

Copyright © 2002
Morning Sun Books, Inc.

All rights reserved. This book may not be reproduced in part or in whole without written permission from the publisher, except in the case of brief quotations or reproductions of the cover for the purposes of review.

Library of Congress
Catalog Card No. 2001-126473

First Printing
ISBN 1-58248-062-1

Published by
Morning Sun Books, Inc.
9 Pheasant Lane
Scotch Plains, NJ 07076
Printed in Korea

Robert J. Yanosey, President
To access our full library In Color visit us at
www.morningsunbooks.com

Acknowledgements

This Morning Sun Color Guide involves two railroads, and as such, this meant that twice as much background work needed to be performed to get it to publication. Therefore, it is even more important that I take this opportunity to express my many thanks for the kind folks who have helped out in many ways to bring this volume to completion: Ralph Barger, Craig Bossler, Bob Hubler, Dick Dawson, Mark Evans, Ed Hawkins, Richard Hendrickson, Roger Hinman, Ed Kaminski, Dan Kohlberg, Tom Madden, Eric Neubauer, John Pitts, Art Richardson, Bob Schramm, Allen Stanley and Charlie Volkar.

I would also like to express my most heartfelt thanks and kudos to the following folks who spent much time with me and provided considerable in-depth help on specific car histories: Ken Donnelly, Gene Glendinning and John Pitts. In addition, many thanks to Dave Wagner for his editing expertise! It is no exaggeration to state that without their help this volume would still be awaiting completion. Thanks guys!

Finally, I'd like to thank Bob Yanosey for his patience with this particular volume in the continuing Morning Sun Color Guide series.

As with all of the Morning Sun Color Guides, this volume simply couldn't have been possible without the generous contributions of photographic material from many kind people and I'd like to take this time to properly give them my thanks. Photos come from the following sources: Arthur Angstadt, Dick Argo, Peter Arnold, Don Ball, Roger Bee, George Berisso, Craig Bossler, Alan Bradley, Glyn Burke, Paul Coe, Conniff Railroadiana Collection, Larry DeYoung, T.J. Donahue, Ken Donnelly, E. Van Dusen, Jim Eager, Melvern Finzer, Bill Folsom, John Furst, W.A. Gibson, Emery Gulash, Matt Herson, Lawson Hill, Steven Johnson, Ray Kucaba, Owen Leander, Bob Markle, George Melvin, Paul Meyer, Melvin Mowrer, Walter Peters, Dr. Art Peterson, Joseph Petric, Ron Plazzotta, Russ Porter, Art Richardson, Howard Robins, Jim Rogers, Lou Schmitz, Jim Selzer, Bob Simons, J.W. Swanberg, Jim Thorington, Bob Trennert, Dave Wagner, Richard Wallin, William White, Bob Wilt, Paul Winters, W. Woelfer, Bernie Wooller, Bob Yanosey and the Boston and Hawk Mountain chapters of the NRHS.

The terms "Center Flow", "ASF and ASF Ride Control", "Barber" and "Airslide" are Registered Trademarks of ACF Industries Incorporated, Amsted Industries, Standard Truck Company Corporation and GATX Corporation respectively and are used in this work for product identification only.

 ## Table of Contents

Illinois Central
```
Passenger . . . . . . . . . . . . . . . . . . . . . . . .4
Box Car . . . . . . . . . . . . . . . . . . . . . . . . .32
Covered Hopper . . . . . . . . . . . . . . . . . . .49
Flat Car . . . . . . . . . . . . . . . . . . . . . . . . .55
Gondola . . . . . . . . . . . . . . . . . . . . . . . .60
Intermodal . . . . . . . . . . . . . . . . . . . . . .63
Refrigerator . . . . . . . . . . . . . . . . . . . . .65
Hopper . . . . . . . . . . . . . . . . . . . . . . . .66
Caboose . . . . . . . . . . . . . . . . . . . . . . .68
Maintenance of Way . . . . . . . . . . . . . .73
```

Gulf, Mobile and Ohio
```
Passenger . . . . . . . . . . . . . . . . . . . . .77
Box Car . . . . . . . . . . . . . . . . . . . . . . .88
Hopper . . . . . . . . . . . . . . . . . . . . . . .101
Covered Hopper . . . . . . . . . . . . . . . .103
Flat Car . . . . . . . . . . . . . . . . . . . . . .108
Refrigerator . . . . . . . . . . . . . . . . . . .111
Gondola . . . . . . . . . . . . . . . . . . . . . .112
Intermodal . . . . . . . . . . . . . . . . . . . .113
Caboose . . . . . . . . . . . . . . . . . . . . . .114
Maintenance of Way . . . . . . . . . . . . .118
```

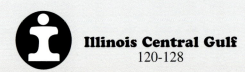

INTRODUCTION

The Illinois Central

The Illinois Central operated some of the most famous, and probably the best looking, passenger trains in America. Chocolate and orange trains such as the CITY OF MIAMI and the CITY OF NEW ORLEANS were just two of their better known passenger trains.

The IC's passenger fleet was being constantly updated and modified for continued service in a changing marketplace. After the road's initial post World War Two passenger car buying spree, few newly built cars were procured, although the road did purchase cars from other roads. The Illinois Central was able to meet the travelling public's needs by virtue of the continual rebuilding and conversions performed at their Chicago Burnside Shops. This work was often as complex as taking an ordinary coach and completely rebuilding it into a streamlined observation car.

This penchant for rebuilding would cause the road to continue to operate a predominately heavyweight fleet in a lightweight era. Too, because of the heavy head end business, the IC also became an early proponent of the FlexiVan concept, an early system of containerized movements.

Unfortunately, this constant rebuilding of older equipment resulted in Amtrak (which took over intercity passenger rail operations on May 1, 1971) disposing of virtually all of the IC's equipment. Although some of the more modern cars continued to operate on an interim basis during the early days of Amtrak, only one car was known to have been purchased outright by Amtrak, although apparently it was never actually used by that firm.

The Illinois Central operated a unique freight car fleet due to the world class car building shops at their Centralia Shops, in Illinois. These shops constructed an amazing variety of cars, most to their own design. Equipment was, of course, also purchased from outside builders, making for a rich variety of designs for the railfan. In addition, the IC also leased cars from National Refrigerator Car, a leasing company which operated refrigerator cars primarily out of the southern ports in support of the fruit and vegetable trade.

Illinois Central cabooses also warrant a closer look due to their side doors, an item not often found on other modern class one roads. These unique looking cabooses were found throughout the system, with the exception of the state of Iowa, which prohibited side door cabooses.

The Gulf, Mobile and Ohio

Although the GM&O was a smaller operator of passenger trains than rival Illinois Central, they did operate such well-known trains as the Abraham Lincoln and Ann Rutledge, all painted in the red and maroon paint scheme.

The GM&O primarily operated passenger equipment acquired from predecessor roads Gulf, Mobile and Northern and the Mobile and Ohio, along with equipment inherited from the Alton (known as the Chicago and Alton prior to B&O control). While much of this heavyweight equipment was fairly standard, the GM&O also operated two nearly identical train sets constructed both in aluminum and steel and featuring full-width diaphragms between cars. An interesting facet to GM&O passenger cars is the fact that their streamlined (i.e., lightweight) coach and parlor cars featured three axle trucks, in the belief that six wheel trucks contributed to smoother riding qualities. Unfortunately, due to age, none of the GM&O's passenger equipment was acquired by Amtrak.

The Gulf, Mobile and Ohio's freight car roster can be summed up with the word: dedicated. This road had a larger percentage of assigned equipment than almost any other. While the road rarely rebuilt cars (either passenger or freight) to the extent that rival IC did, they did have heavy car shops at Frascati Shops in Mobile, Alabama. In addition, additional shops were also located in Meridian, Mississippi and at Bloomington, Illinois.

If anything, the GM&O's caboose fleet was diverse. The GM&O probably had, caboose for caboose, the most diverse fleet of any class one railroad. Cars came from such varying backgrounds as the B&O, Mobile and Ohio and the Gulf, Mobile and Northern. Some could trace their heritage back to the acquisition of the New Orleans Great Northern in 1933!

The Illinois Central Gulf

While not the focus of this volume, we would be remiss not to take a very quick look at the result of the Illinois Central and Gulf, Mobile and Ohio's merger on August 10, 1972. So we've included a small section of freight and business car equipment at the end of this work to illustrate a part of this road's newly formed roster.

There is much on all of these roads worth looking at both for the historian and modeler. We invite you to take a close look at what they had to offer!

ILLINOIS CENTRAL PASSENGER

4

RPO 103, series 95-104
▲ When originally built by Pullman in 1914 under lot 4183, this group of steel 64'0" postal cars featured six windows per side in a split arrangement. At least one car (100) was remodeled in 1935 to incorporate all six windows near one end of the car. Apparently the cars that remained in this class in early 1961 (with 97 & 99 missing) were then rebuilt by the IC's Chicago Burnside Shops to this final configuration, as illustrated here at Chicago's Central Station in July 1963. Note the steel plating astride the doorways to withstand the scuffing endured while catching mailbags on the fly. *(Paul Winters)*

RPO 153, series 150-160
▼ Railway Post Office 153 clatters across the 21st Street interlocking in this May 1967 view taken in Chicago. This car, as does the entire series, has an interesting history. Originally sleeper *City of New Orleans*, built by Pullman in 1941 as lot 6670, it was converted to this configuration in August 1962. The other cars in this series were also converted from sleepers, the conversions beginning in February 1961 and going through April 1965. All of these cars were then later converted yet again to baggage-express cars with RPO 153 being renumbered to 1838 in April 1970. With Amtrak's takeover of intercity passenger service, it would be sold to the Garrett Historical Corporation in Indiana. *(Ron Plazzotta)*

Baggage 510, series 500-519
▲ This "auxiliary" baggage-express car was found sitting at the Spruce Street coach yard in Columbus, Ohio in October 1962. With a rather short uncoupled overall length of 54'6 1/2", these cars were built by ACF under lot 1662 in 1937. Some cars included desks and toilets, others were plain inside. Rated at 3,452 cubic foot capacity, these cars used six foot wide single side doors. They would be retired (with some going into MofW service) in January and February 1968 with the demise of U.S. Mail service (and corresponding train reductions) by the railroad. *(Paul Winters)*

Horse Car 533, series 532-537
▼ This rather unusual car was designed for transporting horses. Built by Standard Steel at Hammond, Indiana in 1924, it was spotted in North Milwaukee in September 1966. In 1941 two cars, 532 and 536, were converted to regular baggage-express cars and renumbered as 810 and 811 (see page 7). These remaining cars had 24 stalls, installed lengthwise to the car, for horses. Note the screened ventilator openings near the doors. The four cars not renumbered were retired in late 1967, with number 533 meeting her demise in December of that year. *(Ron Plazzotta)*

Mail Storage 568, series 565-575

◀ Built by Pullman under lot 4533 in June 1918, this mail storage car was originally IC 744 (these cars being converted from Illinois Central's 740-745 baggage cars). It was spotted in St. Louis in September 1967, still quite active. With the wholesale loss of head end business in the late 1960's, most of these cars were retired in mid 1968 (number 568 in June), although several managed to stay on the roster until the early 1970's.

(Paul Winters)

Baggage-Expresses 713 and 725, series 712-729

▶▲ We couldn't resist showing both old and new paint schemes for this series of cars. Baggage 713 was spotted at the Spruce Street Yard in Columbus, Ohio on December 14, 1962 in green paint (with black roof). Baggage 725, on the other hand, has the much more spectacular brown, orange and yellow paint, certainly brightening up the car! This car, assigned to magazine loading, was photographed in July 1963 at the north end of Chicago's Central Station. Both cars were built by Pullman (lot 4410) in 1916 and 1917. Car 725 would be retired in February 1968; the eventual status of 713 is unknown.

(both, Paul Winters)

Baggage-Express 794, series 790-794

▲ In excellent paint, clerestory roof and all, this baggage-express car sits in Milwaukee, Wisconsin in September 1966. These cars were built by ACF in 1926 under lot 212. With both eight and four feet, ten inch doors, these cars were 73'5 1/2" long uncoupled. Along with numerous other head end cars, these baggage-express car retirements began in late 1967 and continued through 1968. This car was stricken from the roster in April 1968.

(Ron Plazzotta)

Baggage-Express 811, series 810-811

▼ This car was originally built as IC 536 at Standard Steel's Hammond, Indiana plant as lot 2711 in 1924. It originated as part of the horse-car series 532-537 (see page 5 for horse car 533). This cars mate, IC 810, was originally 532. Baggage-express 811 was spotted sitting in St. Louis in April 1968 and gives us a good look at those Harriman roof lines. While the exact disposition of this car is unknown, sister 810 was retired in February 1970.

(Emery Gulash)

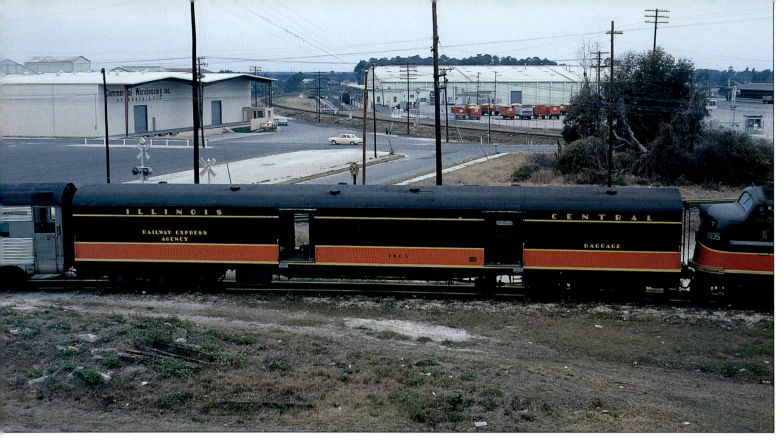

Baggage-Express 1805, series 1804-1805
▲ The background of these cars is quite interesting. These two cars were converted from baggage-dormitory cars 1903-1904 at the road's Burnside Shops in south Chicago. In turn, these two baggage-dormitory cars were themselves conversions from coaches 2200 and 2177 (part of the series 2168-2206, built by Pullman in 1916 as 88 seat coaches), having been converted in 1947 and 1948 for CITY OF NEW ORLEANS service. This excellent view of 1805 was taken in Auburndale, Florida in February 1968. By July 1972, both of these cars would be removed from the Illinois Central's roster. *(Paul Coe)*

Baggage-Express 1832, series 1830-1832
▼ The Illinois Central was very adept in rebuilding cars to suit changing needs. A case in point is this car, shown here in Chicago on August 29, 1971. These three cars began life with the New York Central as part of their *Bay* series of 22 roomette sleepers built by Pullman in 1949 under lot 6790. The Illinois Central acquired several of these cars in 1961. The three cars in this series originated as the NYC's *Little Neck Bay, Manhasset Bay* and *Great South Bay*, which were converted by the Illinois Central's Burnside Shops in 1961 and 1962 to postal-mail storage cars 150-152. Then, in 1968, they were converted yet again to the present configuration as shown here. All three of these cars would be removed from service in July and August 1972. *(Owen Leander)*

Baggage-Dormitory 1900, series 1900
▲ The photographer caught this baggage-dormitory car sitting in the sunshine in Atlanta, Georgia in April 1969. This car was originally built by Pullman under lot 6633 in 1940 as a baggage-dormitory, 22 chair car for the CITY OF MIAMI and was named *Bougainvillea*, but lost its name during a rebuilding in September 1949 which resulted in the car shown here. A nice black and white photo of this car, shown as built with its original orange, green and scarlet paint scheme (along with the train and car name) can be seen in Paul Somers' book *Illinois Central Streamliners, 1936-1946*. In August 1972, this car would be retired and scrapped. *(Bill Folsom)*

Baggage-Dormitory 1906, series 1906
▼ Another baggage-dormitory is this car, shown while backing into Central Station in Chicago. In dedicated CITY OF MIAMI service, this car was converted in 1951 from IC 2202, out of the coach series 2168-2206 (a series which supplied equipment for many of the Illinois Central's conversions and rebuildings over the years). It had a 22 foot baggage area, the rest of the car being used for space for 24 crew bunks along with lockers, showers, etc. With its lack of windows, this car would make for an interesting model. Baggage-dorm 1906 continued in CITY OF MIAMI service right up until the advent of Amtrak, eventually winding up at the Monticello, Illinois Railroad Museum. *(Ron Plazzotta)*

Dome 2202, series 2200-2202

◀ Dome 2202 was found at Central Station, Chicago in May 1969. This car was one of three similar cars purchased from the Missouri Pacific in June 1967. Their MP numbers were 590-592, which were themselves renumberings from the original 890-892 series. These 70 seat (46 lower, 24 in dome) cars were built by Budd under lot 9646-006 in 1948 for Missouri Pacific subsidiary International-Great Northern. These were unusual cars on the Illinois Central with their corrugated stainless steel construction. Notice the painted over dome windows, an attempt to control overheating in the summer. *(Ron Plazzotta)*

Dome 2212, series 2210-2212

▼ The Illinois Central also acquired three other dome cars from the Missouri Pacific in June 1967, but of more conventional (for the Illinois Central anyway) smooth sided low alloy, high tensile steel construction. Dome 2212, illustrating the lines of these cars, was built by Pullman-Standard in 1952 as lot 6904. This group of cars comes from two MP system roads. This dome is ex MP 597, originally delivered as Texas and Pacific 200. The other two domes, IC 2210 and 2211, were ex MP 594 and 596 (originally MP 893 and 896) respectively. With less toilet space below the dome area than the Budd built cars shown above, these cars had seats for 76 passengers (52 lower and 24 in dome). Note that when this car was photographed, the dome windows were still unpainted. Compare this view, taken in Chicago in September 1968 to the view illustrated on page 109 in Lloyd Stagner's *Illinois Central in Color*, by Morning Sun, taken in August 1966. Same place, but note that two new tracks for the St. Charles Air Line have been added. This new trackage allowed IC Iowa Division freight trains to run directly into Markham Yard.

(Ron Plazzotta)

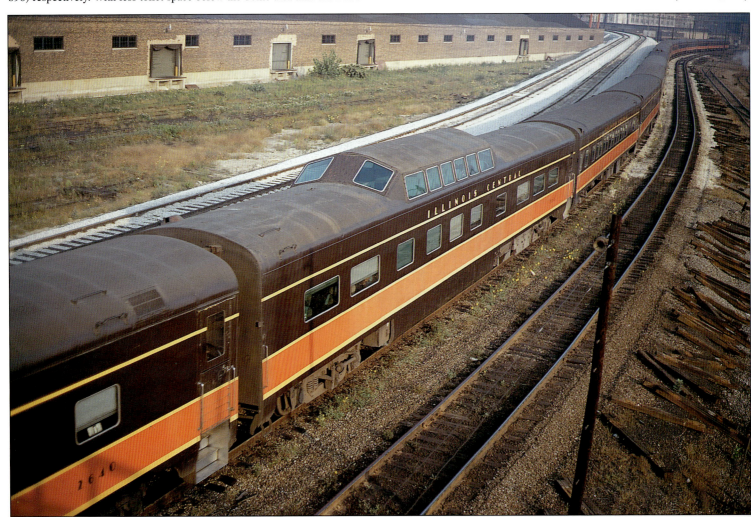

Coach 2602, series 2601-2602

▶ This coach, shown at Chicago's Central Station in August 1968, was originally built by Pullman in 1940 as lot 6633 for CITY OF MIAMI service and named *Hibiscus*. Companion 2601 was named *Japonica*. These cars had 28 rotating and reclining seats plus two bulkhead seats for a total passenger capacity of 60 (although four seats were reserved for the conductor and other train personnel). *Japonica* was wrecked in 1971 while *Hibiscus* would be retired in July 1972 and sold to a private owner. *(Ron Plazzotta)*

Coaches 2623 and 2627, series 2614-2640

▲▼In 1947 Pullman outshopped a group of 56 seat coach cars under lot 6766 for various Illinois Central trains. Coach 2623 was originally named *Tulane* and placed in CITY OF NEW ORLEANS service running from St. Louis to New Orleans. Coach 2627, named *Plaquemine* was also originally assigned to CITY OF NEW ORLEANS service, but running from Louisville to New Orleans. Other assignments for this series were the GREEN DIAMOND and LAND O' CORN trains. Here, we see both sides of these cars at Chicago's Central Station, 2623 in August 1968 and 2627 the following month. In March 1972, coach 2627 would be removed from the roster however the fate of 2623 is unknown. *(both, Ron Plazzotta)*

Coach 2694, series 2692-2694

◀ Coach 2694, a 48 seat car, is shown here at Chicago's 21st Street interlocking in March 1967. This car was rebuilt by the Illinois Central in 1948, as were the other two cars, from the original series 3658-3667. Although the series shows three cars in it, according to the IC's diagram book, coach 2693 was destroyed by fire in Waterloo, Iowa on April 20, 1949. The remaining two cars were placed in general service. Coach 2692 would be retired in March 1972 with this car to follow two months later. *(Ron Plazzotta)*

Coach 2740, series 2735-2740

▶ Although the heading would indicate that this car is part of one overall series numbered 2735 through 2740, the series actually includes five cars from three lots under two builders. This specific car is from Pullman, built under lot 4532 in 1918. Several cars were from ACF in 1912 and others from Pullman in 1919. Coach 2740 has been renumbered several times over the years. It originated as 2243 (part of the series 2232-2256) and was subsequently renumbered to 2913. Eventually it received the present number. A 56 seat coach, it is shown here negotiating the complex trackage at the 21st Street Crossing in Chicago in April 1967. This coach would be withdrawn from service in March 1970.

(Ron Plazzotta)

Coach 2741, series 2741

▼ Originally built by Pullman in 1925 under lot 4858, this car has been renumbered several times. It originated from the 2257-2286 coach series as car 2268, then was remarked 2933. Later on, the car was converted to a coach lounge, number 3800, and then finally restencilled to its present number as shown here in Champaign, Illinois in March 1967. Less than two years later, in January 1969, this car would be retired.

(Alan Bradley)

Coach 2813, series 2813-2818, 2820-2822
▲ This 64 seat coach was found sitting in the IC's Weldon, Chicago coach yard on June 13, 1970. It was part of a mixed bag of cars renumbered several times over the years. This particular car was originally 2237 and renumbered to 2909, thence to 2813. It was built by Pullman in 1918 and was in general service. Many cars from this group left the roster in mid to late 1970. *(Owen Leander)*

Coach 2819, series 2804, 2819
▼ Chicago's Central Station was the location of this car when photographed in January 1969. With a 60 seat capacity, this car originated as IC 2277 (series 2257-2286) and subsequently converted and renumbered to 2703, eventually becoming 2819. It was built by Pullman in 1925 under lot 4858. *(Ron Plazzotta)*

Coach 2859, series 2852-2862

▶ This 64 seat coach was found sitting in Chicago on August 29, 1971. It had been converted from coach 2917, which was itself a conversion from coach 2247 (from the series 2232-2256), built by Pullman as lot 4532 in 1918. *(Owen Leander)*

Coach 2864, series 2863-2864

▲ Another much converted coach is this car, found at Chicago on March 2, 1969. Although listed as a conversion from ex coach 2751 (itself a conversion from 3155, out of the series 3150-3161 built by Pullman as lot 4615 in 1921), it appears that the conversion was mostly internal (apparently including the removal of the women's lounge). Based on available data, the window arrangement remained the same during the conversion. Sister 2863 was ex-2752, nee 3156.

(Owen Leander, Bob Trennert collection)

Coach 2902, series 2902

▼ Apparently a single car conversion, this coach was located in Chicago on September 27, 1969. Like many of the Illinois Central's passenger cars, it has a long and varied history. It originated as coach 3647 from the series 3641-3648, built by ACF as lot 885 in 1929. From there, it was rebuilt/renumbered to car 3305. And then once again, it was renumbered/converted to car 2730. And finally, a last conversion resulted in the car that you see here. As you can see, the Illinois Central was a master in rebuilding equipment over the years to suit changing needs! *(Owen Leander)*

Observation-Bar-Lounge 3305, series 3305-3306
▲ Originally coach 2188 (from the series 2168-2206) this observation-bar-lounge was converted by the railroad for CITY OF NEW ORLEANS service in 1947. At the time it was named *Mardi Gras*, while its companion, 3306 (originally coach 2175) was named *Audubon Park*. Here it sits at Champaign, Illinois in November 1967. The small door amidships was for bar servicing. Observation seating was for 21, while the lounge seated 27 passengers. Companion 3306 left the roster in January 1969 with 3305 going to the Roanoke Chapter of the NRHS in August of that year. *(Alan Bradley)*

Observation-Bar-Lounge 3309, series 3309
▼ Rebuilt for mid train service, this observation-bar-lounge sits at Springfield, Illinois on August 18, 1965. Built by Pullman under lot 4519 in 1916 as coach 2187 (from the series 2168-2206, which provided cars for many rebuildings and conversions), this car was converted by the railroad's south Chicago Burnside Shops in 1952. Note the blunt ended design of this car, quite a difference from the more traditional boat tail design of the car shown above. In the late 1960's, the railroad began painting the observation ends of the cars solid brown. A 42 seat car, it left the roster in December 1971. *(Richard Wallin, Matt Herson collection)*

Observation-Parlor 3312 -Gulfport, series 3312

▶ In 1942, Pullman delivered two twin bedroom, two compartment, one drawing room sleeper-observation cars for the PANAMA LIMITED under lot 6672. One car was named *Memphis* and the other *Gulfport* (seen on page 24). After removal from Pullman lease service, and after rebuilding to observation-parlor status, *Gulfport* was assigned Illinois Central number 3312 on September 1, 1966. In this view, *Gulfport* sits in New Orleans, Louisiana on April 21, 1964 complete with its PANAMA LIMITED signboard on the boat tail. *Gulfport* would be retired in April 1968. *(George Berisso)*

Observation-Tavern-Lounge 3314, series 3314

▲ Sitting along US 55 in Illinois on August 30, 1974, observation-tavern-lounge 3314 shows of her lines from an extensive rebuilding for mid train service in December 1963. Originally IC 3311, this car was a boat tail observation-parlor car built by Pullman in 1948 under lot 6799. As built, this car was assigned to GREEN DIAMOND service. Obs 3314 seated 24 in the forward lounge area and 23 in the aft lounge area at the observation end of the car. This car left the railroad's roster in December 1971. *(Owen Leander)*

Observation-Bar-Lounge 3320, series 3320

▼ Showing off her classic boat tail lines in Chicago on March 2, 1969 (possibly in a dead line as this car left the roster sometime in March 1969), obs-bar-lounge 3320 was in general service. It was rebuilt by the railroad in 1947 from coach 2173 (built by Pullman in 1916) and subsequently had her interior remodeled in 1951. When originally rebuilt in 1947, it acquired the name *Paducah*, (though it had lost this name by the time of the photo) and was assigned to the Louisville-Fulton, Kentucky run. This car seated 21 patrons in the observation portion while another 19 could be accommodated in the lounge. *(Owen Leander)*

Parlor 3350, series 3350

▶ This nice view, taken in Chicago's Weldon Coach Yard at an unrecorded date, illustrates the lines of this 40 seat parlor car. Originally built as coach 3160 by Pullman in 1921, it had been converted by the railroad in 1948 for PANAMA LIMITED Chicago to Carbondale service. At the time of the conversion it was named *Illini*, running north in the morning and back south in the evening. *(Bill Folsom)*

Sleeper 3501-*Belleville*, series 3500-3505

▲ In July 1953, Pullman built this eleven double bedroom car as lot 6913 for the Pullman company. In 1969, when the railroad assigned car numbers to these sleeping cars apparently they also opted to update the paint scheme with the "Big Image" paint scheme, featuring the new split-rail logo and more simplistic lettering graphics. *Belleville*, shown here in Chicago on October 3, 1970, would be pulled off the roster in September of the following year. *(Owen Leander)*

Sleeper 3503-*Bloomington*, series 3500-3505

▼ *Bloomington* sits somewhere in southern California (probably in the Los Angeles Union Station coach yard) in this December 1972 view. While *Bloomington* is likely in interim Amtrak service, few, if any, IC passenger cars were purchased for active Amtrak service. It is from the same series as the car shown just above, but here we see the opposite, corridor side of the car. Note that along with the "Big Image" paint scheme, there is an ACI label attached to the cars' side. Most of these cars left the roster in late 1971.

(Matt Herson collection)

Sleeper 3517-*Clifton*, series 3510-3522
▲ In late 1950 and early 1951, the Illinois Central acquired eight, ten roomette, six double bedroom sleeping cars from the Chesapeake and Ohio Railroad. Here we see *Clifton* at Ocala, Florida in March 1969. It would be numbered as IC's 3517 sometime in 1969, although apparently not by the time this photo was taken. *Clifton* was acquired in November 1950 and was the C&O's *City of Marion*, built by Pullman in 1949 as lot 6864. *(Bob Yanosey collection)*

Sleeper 3530-*Cook County*, series 3525-3532
▼ In June 1965, the Illinois Central acquired eight more ten roomette, six double bedroom sleepers, this time from the Nickel Plate Road. Again, in 1969, numbers were assigned. *Cook County*, shown here at some unrecorded location in August 1969, was originally NKP's *City of Peoria*. These cars originated at Pullman in 1950 under lot 6866. *(Paul Coe)*

Sleeper 3535-*Magnolia State*, series 3535-3536
▲ In April 1942, Pullman built twelve, six roomette, six section, four double bedroom sleepers for PANAMA LIMITED service as lot 6669. By the time *Magnolia State* was found sitting in Chicago on September 27, 1969, only two of these cars remained; *Magnolia State* and *Banana Road*. In 1969, both cars received numbers assigned by the railroad, although obviously this car hadn't been so marked by the date of this photo. Indeed, *Magnolia State* never did get a number stencilled in the little time remaining for this car (as both cars were retired in March of the following year). *(Owen Leander)*

Diner 4100-*Palm Garden*, series 4100
▼ Built by Pullman-Standard for CITY OF MIAMI service in 1940 as lot 6633 and named *Palm Garden*, diner 4100 sits faded and weatherworn along US 55 in Illinois on August 30, 1974, a far cry from its heyday when it was painted in the original CITY OF MIAMI orange, green and scarlet colors. Retired from the railroad since December 1971, diner 4100 was sold to Amendment Lounge at Shorewood, Illinois. *(Owen Leander)*

Diner-Lounge 4105, series 4105
▲ Diner-lounge 4105 sits in Chicago Illinois on June 13, 1970 with her new Illinois Central logo and graphics. This car is another excellent example of the IC's ability to get the most out of her equipment. It began life as diner 3998, from the series 3990-3999, built by Pullman in 1916 as lot 4408. It was then rebuilt and renumbered to 4151 in 1947. Yet another rebuilding resulted in the car illustrated here. The dining room had a capacity for 32 patrons and the lounge another ten. *(Owen Leander)*

Diner-Lounge 4111, Series 4111
▼ Another converted car is diner-lounge 4111, found sitting in Chicago's Central Station in August 1969. Assigned to pool service, it began service with the railroad as diner 3987, from the series 3985-3989, built by Pullman as lot 4733 in 1923. This particular car was then converted and renumbered in 1948. Seating was for 32 passengers in the dining section and a further ten in the lounge area. *(Ron Plazzotta)*

Diner-Lounge 4112, series 4112
▲ In November 1962, the Illinois Central purchased this diner-lounge from the Chicago and Eastern Illinois, where it had been their number 505. It was built by Pullman-Standard in 1946 under lot 6743. In this view, we see the car in Illinois Central colors on a beautiful day in September 1968 on the move in Chicago. While on the C&EI this car was a straight diner but apparently the IC converted it to seat 24 patrons in a dining area and another 16 in the lounge (although the seating arrangements were flexible). In July 1970, this car would be retired from IC service. *(Ron Plazzotta)*

Diner 4175, series 4175-4176
▼ In 1950, the Illinois Central acquired two twin unit diner-kitchen/dorm cars from the Chesapeake and Ohio for PANAMA LIMITED service. They were built by Pullman-Standard in 1950 under lot 6860 and had seating for 56 patrons. When acquired from the C&O, these diners were numbered from C&O 1973 and 1974 to IC 4125 and 4126. Upon their rebuilding by the railroad in March and April 1967, the cars were renumbered into the series shown here. This diner, coupled to mate kitchen/dorm 4175A (illustrated on the next page), was found in Chicago in August 1969 some three months prior to its retirement. *(Paul Coe)*

Kitchen-Dormitory 4175A, series 4175A-4176A
▲ The mate to the full dining car 4175, shown on the prior page, is illustrated in this view, also taken in Chicago in August 1969. Like their dining car mates, the two cars in this series were also built by Pullman-Standard in 1950 for the C&O, being built under lot 6859. When acquired by the Illinois Central for PANAMA LIMITED service, they were renumbered from C&O 1950 and 1951 to IC 4125A and 4126A. Also rebuilt by the Illinois Central in April and May 1967, they then received their new IC numbers 4175A and 4176A. There were provision for 16 crew sleeping berths in this car along with a full kitchen and pantry. *(Paul Coe)*

Sleeper *Galena*, series *Galena* and *Gilman*
▼ In late 1958, the Illinois Central acquired a number of sleeping cars from the New York Central Railroad, from several different NYC groups. Two cars, built as ten roomette, six double bedroom sleepers, were originally the NYC's *Brooklyn Bridge* and *Eads Bridge*. Upon the transfer, the IC renamed *Brooklyn Bridge* to *Galena* and *Eads Bridge* to *Gilman* (shown on the next page). In this view, we see *Galena* in Chicago, Illinois on September 2, 1968. In two months, this car would be retired from the railroad. *(Owen Leander)*

Sleeper *Gilman*, series *Galena* and *Gilman*
▲ As noted on the prior page, when this car (along with mate *Galena*) was acquired in November 1958 from the NYC, it was repainted and renamed for a junction point in northern Illinois. Originally the New York Central's *Eads Bridge* this four compartment, four double bedroom, two drawing room car was spotted in Chicago on July 13, 1968. In this view, we take a look at the opposite side of one of the cars in this series. These cars were built by Pullman in 1938 under lot 6540. Like *Galena, Gilman* would be retired from service in December 1968. *(Owen Leander)*

Sleeper *Hammond*, series *Greenville*, *Grenada*, *Hammond* and *Harvey*
▼ Another group of sleeping cars was acquired by the railroad in late 1958 and October 1960 from the NYC. One car acquired in October 1960 was the New York Central's *Imperial Dome*, shown here in IC colors and renamed *Hammond*. These cars were built by Pullman in 1940 as lot 6617 and were also four compartment, four double bedroom, two drawing room sleepers. *Hammond* was found in Chicago on March 3, 1968. She would be retired two months after this photograph was taken. *(Owen Leander)*

 Observation *Memphis*, series *Gulfport* and *Memphis*
▲ Built by Pullman in 1941 as lot 6672 for PANAMA LIMITED service, *Memphis* and *Gulfport* were two bedroom, two compartment, one drawing room, lounge-observation cars. Lounge capacity was 17 while another eight patrons could be accomodated in the observation area. *Gulfport*, rebuilt in September 1966, can be seen on page 16. Here we see *Memphis* at the north end of Chicago's Central Station in July 1963. While *Gulfport* would eventually be assigned a number by the railroad, apparently *Memphis* never did acquire one (and thus its showing here, in the named car section of this book). *Memphis* would suffer a derailment accident on July 5, 1965 and subsequently be retired at Markham Yard on November 8th of that year. *(Paul Winters)*

▼ Our last revenue passenger car is this scene from years gone by. In this idyllic scene, one of the Illinois Central's observation cars sits at the end of the track at New Orleans in 1953. What we wouldn't give to be there, getting ready to depart on another fast run on one of the Illinois Central's classic streamliners? *(T.J. Donahue)*

Business car 1

▲ Probably one of the more famous business cars, this President's car was one of the last to be supplied to a railroad for such service. Built as a shell by Pullman-Standard in 1956 (as lot 6971), it was finished by the railroad at their Burnside Shops. Nice interior and mid completion photos can be found in *The Official Pullman-Standard Library, Volume 12*, by Randall and Anderson. In this photo, we see this car in Memphis on April 28, 1969 still very much at work on the Illinois Central. Like most business cars, this was a self contained car with a kitchen, porter's room, dining area (for ten), five bedrooms and the observation area.

(William White photo, Bill Folsom collection)

Business car 6

▼ Assigned to the Vice President of Operations, business car 6 sits in Chicago on June 13, 1970. This car was built by ACF as lot 7477 in 1915 as business car number 16. Like the President's car above, this car contained a kitchen and porter's quarters. Dining service was for eight however and there were only three sleeping areas (two state rooms and a secretary's room). Also like business car number 1, there were provisions for an additional guest's bed in the observation area via a sofa-berth. It is interesting to find that diagram sheet notes indicate that this car will not meet NYC clearances and that at 192,000 lbs., one of the heaviest cars on the IC. *(Owen Leander)*

Business car 8
▲ The Vice President-Chief Engineer's car sits at Chicago's Central Station in June 1967. This car, built at Pullman as lot 4466 in 1917, was originally business car 3, then renumbered to US4. At some point in time it was renumbered again to business car 18 and then yet once again (in 1940) renumbered to its present number, 8. Business car 8 utilized a layout similar to 6, shown on the prior page, but apparently lacked the hide-a-bed/couch-berth sleeping accommodations in the observation area. *(Ron Plazzotta)*

Business car 9
▼ Not every business car was permanently assigned to an individual or an office. Witness this car, found at Chicago's 12th Street Station on May 2, 1958. Built by Pullman under lot 4466 in 1917, it was in general pool service. Although manufactured under the same lot as business car 8 (above), note the many variations between the two cars. And also like business car 8, this car has been renumbered several times over the years. Originally built as IC 15, it then was renumbered to business car 67, then back to 15, then off to the Number One spot and (finally) to its number as seen here. As an interesting aside, when President Wayne Johnston had this car he named it after his children: *Bette-Junior*. *(Eugene Van Dusen)*

Business car 27

▲▼ Our last business car is a bit of a mystery. While I was unable to locate any definitive data on it, I believe that it is renumbered from IC 7. Close observation of these slides (taken at Chicago's Weldon Coach Yard on June 28 and 29, 1969) shows some evidence of new paint at the location of the car's number. In addition, the Illinois Central had previously sold business car 7 on January 18, 1968. These two items, plus the fact that this car's window arrangement exactly matches the this car is likely renumbered from that car. If true, then this car is a sister to business car 8, (shown on the previous page) built by Pullman in 1917 under lot 4466. Assigned to the vice president of traffic, it featured two state rooms, a secretary's room and an eight place dining area and associated kitchen along with a porters room. The observation area seated six and also had a sofa with an upper berth above it.

(both, Owen Leander)

ACL 247, ACL series 228-247
▲ Coach 247, though a bit timeworn and dirty, shows off her Illinois Central paint scheme in Chicago on September 16, 1972. The only coach from this ACL series to be so painted, it was built by Pullman-Standard in 1949 under lot 6808. This 54 seat coach was placed in CITY OF MIAMI service. Interestingly, the other cars in this series were of an identical layout but constructed of corrugated stainless steel side sheathing. Coach 247 would be renumbered as SCL 5469 and eventually wind up with Amtrak with that same number. *(Owen Leander)*

SCL 5478, ex-ACL 248-250
▼ Here is a Seaboard Coast Line coach after its renumbering by the railroad after the ACL-Seaboard merger. This car was built by Pullman-Standard in 1954 as lot 6919 and painted for CITY OF MIAMI service. Like the car just above this was the only car with smooth steel sheathing (specifically for IC service) with the others in the series having corrugated stainless steel sheathing. Originally numbered ACL 248 (a builder's portrait may be seen on page 27 of the *ACL Color Guide to Freight and Passenger Equipment* by Morning Sun), this 54 seat coach car was spotted at an unrecorded location on July 30, 1972. It would eventually go on into Amtrak service under the same number.
(Lawson Hill photo, Boston Chapter, NRHS collection)

ACL 1118, ACL series 1116-1130
▲ The Atlantic Coast Line contributed several coaches for joint SEMINOLE service, which ran between Chicago and Jacksonville. At least two cars from this ACL series were painted in IC colors for this service. ACL 1118 is shown here coupled to 1123 at Albany, Georgia in June 1969. (A nice view of 1123 can be seen on page 24 of the *ACL Color Guide to Freight and Passenger Equipment*.) By this point in time, these cars were likely out of service as the SEMINOLE was discontinued on June 3rd of that year. These cars were built by Bethlehem Steel Car Company in 1938 and were 56 seat coaches. *(Howard Robins)*

UP *Imperial Bird*
UP *Imperial* series
▼ On August 24, 1955 Union Pacific's *Imperial Bird* sits in Oakland, California. Built by Pullman-Standard in 1941 under lot 6668, this car was a four bedroom, four compartment, two drawing room sleeping car. While painted in IC colors, note that the paint scheme is a little bit non standard as the name placement is not typical for the IC and that top stripe is too low. Nonetheless, a fine looking car! *(Lawson Hill photo, Boston Chapter, NRHS collection)*

CofG 663, CofG series 660-663
▶ The Central of Georgia also contributed cars to the joint IC-ACL-CofG (and one-time FEC) CITY OF MIAMI trains. One contribution was this 56 seat coach spotted at a southern location in April 1968. The cars from this Central of Georgia series were built by ACF in 1947 as lot 2866. *(Ron Plazzotta)*

Algoma Central 511
▼ Few, if any, IC passenger cars went into Amtrak service. Most were declared surplus and disposed of although not all Illinois Central passenger cars were cut up as these two views illustrate. Algoma Central was the owner of coach 511, found in Soo, Ontario in August 1980. It originated as a 44 seat coach-grill from the IC series 3341-3345. These were acquired from the Missouri Pacific (ex-564-568) and were built by ACF in 1948 as lot 2881. *(Howard Robins)*

Sonora-Baja-California 5129
▶ Somewhere south of the border, Sonora-Baja-California 5129 sits in the sunshine on February 1, 1974. It is from the Illinois Central 2500-2506 series, built by Pullman-Standard in 1945 and 1946 as lot 6743. These cars were originally ex-C&EI coaches 460-466, purchased by the railroad in 1961. Records show at least some of these coaches left the Illinois Central in late 1971 and early 1972.

(Ron Plazzotta)

Suburban Motor 1118, series 1100-1229
▲ Technically speaking, this Color Guide is primarily intended as a showcase for non powered rolling stock, but as the Illinois Central operated a large fleet of commuter equipment, I thought it appropriate to show one of the classic motor cars in this service. Here we find suburban motor 1118 sitting pans down at Chicago's 18th Street MU yard in May 1972. These venerable cars were built by Pullman in 1926 as lot 4866. This suburban motor car had a capacity of 84 commuters. Some excellent in service scenes of these cars are presented in Morning Sun's *Illinois Central in Color*, by Lloyd Stagner.
(Howard Robins)

Suburban Trailer 1430, series 1346-1430
▼ To go along with the suburban motor cars purchased during the IC's electrification project of the mid 1920's, the railroad ordered 140 trailer cars from both Pullman and Standard Steel. Standard Steel furnished the 85 cars in this series (under lot P3050) in 1926. The other trailers, built by Pullman and which filled out the entire 1301-1440 number series, were built in 1921, 1926 and 1928, all to this same 84 seat design. Trailer 1430 was found under catenary on April 10, 1971 in Chicago.
(Owen Leander)

ILLINOIS CENTRAL BOX CAR

Box Car 3070, series 3000-3999
▲ Our first Illinois Central freight car is this 40'6" box car, built at the IC's Centralia Shops in 1957. In addition to this group of cars, two more batches of similar cars were built in 1957 as IC 4000-4899 and 4900-4999. The latter series included DF loaders. Box car 3070 was found in East St. Louis on November 9, 1980. Although a bit timeworn, note that it still retains its running boards (and original paint), pretty unusual for a car at such a late date. These cars used eight foot Superior doors along with Equipco handbrakes and were rated at 50 ton or 3,898 cu.ft. capacity Note the Pullman-Standard ends (Pullman doors were also installed on cars 3900-3999).
(Ron Plazzotta photo, Ray Kucaba collection)

Box Car 10081, series 10000-10199
▼ Assigned back to the Illinois Central at New Orleans, this car sits at Las Vegas, Nevada on May 18, 1977. Built at Centralia in 1964, these cars featured ten foot Superior doors and three partial Evans DF-2 belt rails. Keystone 20 inch cushion underframes were utilized on these cars, which had an inside length of 50'6" and a capacity of 4,967 cu.ft. That small stencilling mark in the lower right hand corner of the door indicates that this car incorporated nailable steel flooring as did this entire series. In addition, apparently this car had recently had lading band anchors added as indicated by the circle with a vertical line within it on the door. Ajax brand handbrakes finished off these cars. *(Peter Arnold collection)*

Box Car 10345, series 10200-10499
▲ Assigned to paper loading, box car 10345 sits at an unrecorded location in July 1979. This car was part of a series built at Centralia in 1965 and 1966 (this car in January 1966). This group of cars had four DF-2 belts installed along with adjustable doorway bars to better secure these easily damaged loads. Noncushioned, they had ten foot Youngstown doors and nailable steel floors. Rated at 70 ton or 4,966 cu.ft. capacity, Ellcon-National handbrakes were installed. *(Peter Arnold collection)*

Box Car 10530, series 10500-10799
▼ Another series of cars built by the Centralia shops were these cars, out-shopped in 1966. At 50'6" inside length and sporting an eight foot Superior door, box car 10530 sits in San Luis Obispo, California on September 10, 1981. These were rather plain cars, lacking any interior loading equipment. Floors were laminated wood and one of two handbrakes were installed: Universal brand on 10500-10599 and Ajax on 10600-10799. Capacity of this series was 70 ton or 4,967 cu.ft. *(Peter Arnold)*

Box car 10898, series 10800-10899
▲ Although faded and paint splattered, this car has managed to keep its Centralia applied paint up until this November 5, 1983 photo date. Built in 1966 this car was found sitting in Forest View, Illinois. Uncushioned, these cars utilized Miner handbrakes and Superior ten foot doors along with ASF Ride Control trucks. Inside, nine Evans DF-2 belt rails were installed along with doorway bars. In addition, the floor was a 50,000 pound rated National Steel brand nailable steel floor. The capacity of this car was 70 ton or 4,967 cu.ft. *(Ray Kucaba)*

Box Car 11162, series 11000-11299
▼ In nearly new paint, box car 11162 sits in the sunshine at Council Bluffs, Iowa on August 13, 1967. Built at Centralia in April of that year, it was equipped with nine DF-2 belt rails along with adjustable door bars. Inside this uncushioned car was a 50,000 pound National Steel nailable steel floor. Outside, a Universal model 7400 handbrake was installed as were ten foot Youngstown doors and Barber S-2-C trucks. These cars were rated at either 70 ton or 4,952 cu.ft. capacity. *(Lou Schmitz)*

Box Car 11353, series 11300-11499

▶ Only three months old, ACF built box car 11353 was spotted in Chicago in June 1967. Built under lot 11-06139, this Precision Design car incorporated four DF-2 belt rails, adjustable door bars, 50,000 pound nailable steel floors and a Keystone 20 inch cushion underframe. Ten foot Youngstown doors, ASF trucks and a Miner handbrake were also installed. These were 70 ton capacity cars rated at 4,920 cu.ft. *(Ron Plazzotta)*

Box Car 11644, series 11500-11799

▲ Built at Centralia in June 1967, this plug door equipped car was photographed in March 1972. These cars were fitted with four Evans DF-2 belt rails. Uncushioned and rated at either 70 ton or 4,984 cu.ft. capacity, this series also used Miner handbrakes. While these cars had wood floors, the brand varied as did the truck designs. After the merger, the ICG would replace the plug doors on this series with Evans sliding doors. *(Paul Winters)*

Box car 12598, series 12000-12622

▼ Pullman-Standard supplied this car (which we assume was much cleaner at delivery!) in 1967 under their lot 9288 (12100-12622) and 9289 (12000-12099). There were a number of differences between the two lots. Lot 9288 featured ASF Ride Control trucks along with four SL-2 belt rails. Cars delivered under lot 9289 used Barber S-2-C trucks and had nine SL-2 belt rails. Lot 9288 cars used either Universal or Equipco handbrakes while lot 9289 cars were all Universal brand. Youngstown doors and 50,000 pound nailable steel floors were used throughout. This example was found in Cicero, Illinois on September 7, 1985. *(Ray Kucaba)*

Box Car 12741, series 12700-12899
▲ General American built this car in March 1968 under lot BO-8399-A. This group of cars, rated at 70 ton or 4,967 cu.ft. capacity, came with Keystone 20 inch cushioning and Barber S-2-C trucks. Besides the ten foot Superior doors, these cars had four SL-2 belt rails installed along with adjustable door bars and nailable steel flooring. This car was spotted at an unrecorded location two months after delivery. Note the large "no step" notation on the center sill. *(Bob Wilt)*

Box Car 12981, series 12900-13099
▼ Sitting in the Las Vegas, Nevada sunshine in July 1977, this waffle sided box car was assembled at Centralia in December 1969. Although the four continuous DF-2 belt rail waffles are obvious also furnished with the car were 108 lading band anchors along with continuous lading band anchors in the doorway area. There certainly wasn't any excuse for lading to not be tied down securely in these cars! Keystone 20 inch cushioning and Universal brand handbrakes were fitted as were ten foot Youngstown doors. Trucks varied between ASF and Barber designs. A 70 ton capacity car it was also rated at 5,024 cu.ft. *(Peter Arnold collection)*

Box Car 13426, series 13400-13599
◀ In November 1969, the Centralia shops built this 5,024 cu.ft., 70 ton capacity car. This series of cars came furnished with nine DF-2 belt rails and Ajax handbrakes. Noncushioned, they rode on ASF Ride Control trucks. Youngstown ten foot doors finished this car design. With the melting ice making for some unusual markings, Illinois Central 13426 sits in the cold on February 20, 1977 at Cicero, Illinois. *(Ray Kucaba)*

Box Cars 15734 and 15800, series 15500-15999
▲▼ On October 2, 1977, Centralia-built box car 15734 was found sitting in Broadview, Illinois, while 15800 was spotted in Cicero, Illinois on April 3, 1977. These cars were built in March 1960. Cars in the number series 15850-15999 incorporated nine Sparton Tri-Belt loader rails and doorway bars while the remainder apparently had the option of having loaders installed. As can be seen, 15800 has markings showing Sparton Easy Loaders installed. Door designs were split with cars 15500-15509 and 15760-15999 utilizing a Superior design and the others (in series 15510-15759) using the Youngstown version. These 50 ton capacity cars were rated at 4,003 cu.ft. *(both, Ray Kucaba)*

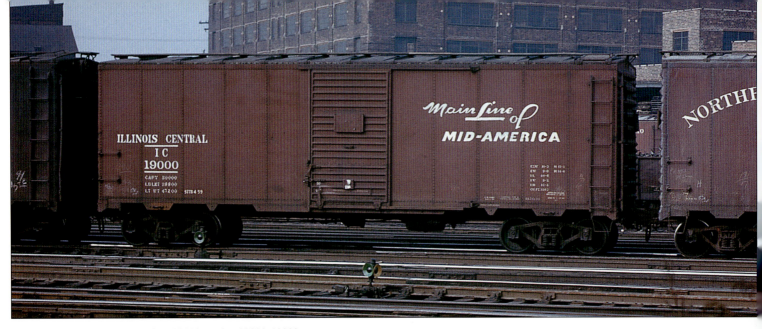

Box Car 19000, series 19000-19999
▲ Class car 19000 sits east of 47th Street in Columbus, Ohio on January 19, 1963. This car was the forerunner of four separate orders for similar cars from ACF and Mt. Vernon Car. The group that includes this car was built at ACF's St. Louis plant in 1939 and 1940 (this car in December 1939) as a 40 ton capacity car with a 3,863 cu.ft. rating. Youngstown six foot doors were installed. As these cars acquired 50 ton trucks, they received new numbers by prefixing the existing ones with the numeral "1". *(Paul Winters)*

Box Cars 23322 and 23466, series 22000-23474
▲▼ Box car 23322, still sporting her original paint (and running boards) when seen at an unrecorded location in June 1973, was built by Centralia in June 1954. Sister 23466 was photographed in February 1968 (showing off the new split rail logo but minus her running boards) and built in December of that same year. Other similar cars were also built at Centralia, both in 1954 and 1955, and placed in the series 23475 through 23534. While not marked with the symbol, these two cars (indeed all of the cars in the series 23000-23534) incorporated 56 lading strap anchors. Six foot Youngstown doors were installed as were Pullman-Standard ends. These 50 ton capacity cars were rated at 3,898 cu.ft. *(both, Paul Winters)*

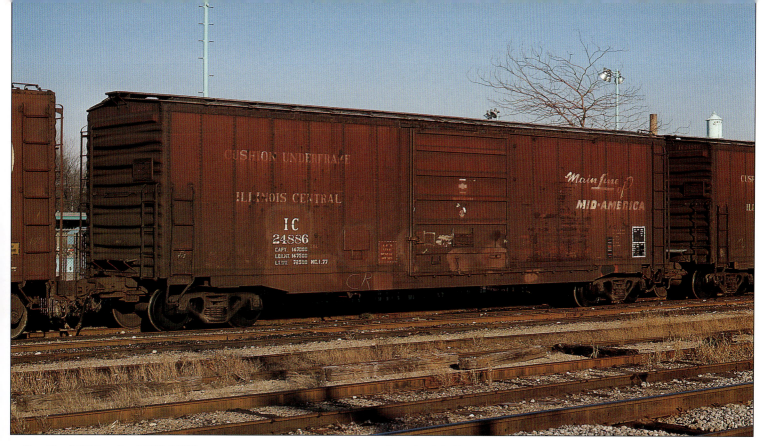

Box Car 24886, series 24700-24899
▲ This Centralia-built car is featured sitting in Broadview, Illinois on November 14, 1977. As denoted by the "cushion underframe" stencilling, it was equipped with a Keystone 20 inch cushioning system (although the last car in this series had a Buckeye 20 inch cushioning system). These cars were built in 1963 and utilized ten foot Superior doors and Sparton Easy Loaders while Universal brand handbrakes were also applied. Capacities were either 4,967 cu.ft. or 70 ton. *(Ray Kucaba)*

Box Car 25143, series 25000-25899
▼ With paint only a month old, box car 25143 sits in Huntsville, Alabama in June 1967. Built at Centralia in 1956, this series was the forerunner of an even larger group of cars making the final number series 25000-26999. The group of cars that 25143 came from included Superior eight foot doors (26000-26999 used Youngstown) and had plain interiors (although 25900-26099 used DF belt rails). Ajax handbrakes were also applied to these cars. *(Bernie Wooller)*

Box Car 28507, series 28000-28999

▶ This rather large series of cars was built by General American with this particular car being built in November 1940. A plain car it used six foot Youngstown doors and had a capacity of 3,863 cu.ft. Box car 28507 was seen in Huntsville, Alabama in June 1967. *(Bernie Wooller)*

Box Car 31920, series 30500-31999

▲ Another rather plain box car is this Centralia built car spotted in July 1969 also in Huntsville, Alabama. It was built in October 1948 and uses Superior doors. Note that the running boards have been removed on this car resulting in the attendant yellow warning placard next to the ladder. This car had been repainted in November of the prior year at the McComb, Mississippi shops with Mobil paint. *(Bernie Wooller)*

Box Car 34730, no series

▼ The background of this car is a little confusing. When restencilled at the McComb, Mississippi shops in March 1963, based on the permanently closed six foot door and lack of end doors, it likely originated from the IC series 34990-34999. These cars were themselves renumbered from the series 38000-38009, which were in turn renumbered from the original series 162301-162400, built at Pullman-Standard's Michigan City, Indiana plant in 1926 as lot 5413. When this car was photographed at some unknown location in June 1966, it was likely in hide service although not so marked. Cars in the 34000 series, a more or less random assemblage of cars, were condemned to hide, tankage and fish loading - a last hurrah for these cars. *(Bill Folsom)*

Box Car 37643, series 37500-37699

▲ Manufactured by Pullman-Standard in May 1967, this box car sits in the former Seaboard Air Line yard in Birmingham, Alabama in July 1968. Built under Pullman's lot 9220, it was equipped with Youngstown ten foot sliding doors and auxiliary six foot plug doors. These 70 ton capacity cars were rated at 4,947 cu.ft. and came fitted with Barber S-2-C trucks and Miner model D-3290-XL handbrakes. *(Jim Thorington)*

Box Car 39551, series 39536-39599

▼ This Centralia-built auto parts car was spotted at Ft. Meade Junction, Maryland in March 1989 with its paint still nicely intact. It was built in 1966 and as stated on the side had a cushion system (Keystone 20 inch) installed. Not so obvious is the Ajax handbrake. The ten foot doors were by Superior. Various interior fittings were installed depending on the individual car. Because of the various interior fittings (or lack of), these cars were AAR classed as XM, XL or XP. *(Jim Rogers)*

Box Car 39654, series 39600-39899

▶ Another Centralia car is this double door car spotted in May 1972. Built in May 1966, it features seven and eight foot Superior doors and has nailable steel flooring installed inside. Note the lack of running boards and short ladder on the right hand side of the car, the result of a then new ruling to delete these items on new or rebuilt house cars. These 70 ton capacity cars were rated at 4,967 cu.ft. *(Paul Winters)*

Box Car 40236, series 40200-40249

▲ When spotted in Greenville, Mississippi on July 10, 1968, this car had been assigned to woodchip service and was to be returned to the IC at Vicksburg when empty. Built by Mt. Vernon Car in October 1929 under lot 7343, it was from a series originally numbered 163151-163200 and AAR classed XAF. These cars came with end doors along with four and six foot side doors, although the side doors were apparently removed and permanent blocking installed for woodchip service. When new, they employed Universal brand handbrakes. While this car had a capacity of 4,284 cu.ft., when new it was only rated at 40 ton. By the time of this photo, it had been upgraded to a 50 ton capacity car. *(George Berisso)*

Box Car 43669, series 43350-43699

▼ Unlike the exotic car shown above, this is a rather plain car found far from home rails at San Luis Obispo, California on April 9, 1981. This car was built at the railroad's Centralia Shops in October 1963 and has a 70 ton capacity. Noncushioned, these cars came with 15' Youngstown doors (seven and eight foot) and nailable steel flooring. With a volume of 4,988 cu.ft., these cars also used Universal brand handbrakes. *(Peter Arnold)*

Box Car 43902, series 43800-43906

▶ The Illinois Central went to Thrall Car and Manufacturing Company for these 60' auto parts cars in 1965. This car, assigned to the Erie at Mansfield, Ohio, was built in June of that year. These were oversized cars exceeding AAR Plate C clearances and had capacities of either 70 ton or 6,367 cu.ft. This car, with its markings noting the Keystone 20 inch cushion underframe that was installed, was found in East Hazelcrest, Illinois on May 26, 1989. Ten foot Youngstown doors were applied as were Miner handbrakes while inside 22 Evans DF-1 belt rails were installed. *(Ray Kucaba)*

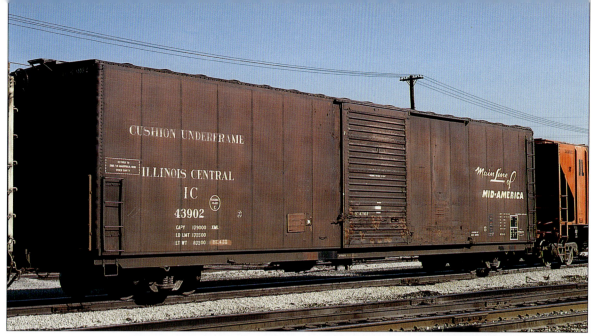

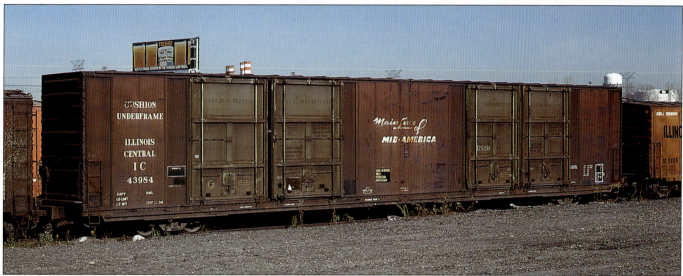

Box Car 43984, series 43907-43949

▲ Thrall Car also supplied this very different car to the Illinois Central in December 1964. This monster (at 86'6" inside length) car was used for lightweight auto parts such as stampings and was found in Forest View, Illinois on November 5, 1983. These cars were fitted with Keystone 20 inch cushion underframes and Universal brand handbrakes. Youngstown aluminum plug doors were also installed, eight per car, as per General Motors' request. Inside, five DF-2 belt rails and two one piece bulkheads were fitted. Unlike most cars, truck mounted "NYCOPAC" brakes were used, eliminating most of the brake rodding often seen below cars. These were truly big cars at AAR Plate F+ clearances! *(Ray Kucaba)*

Box Car 44369, series 44330-44399

▼ This auto parts car was manufactured at the Centralia shops in 1969. With its split-rail emblem and twin eight foot Youngstown doors it was spotted at an unknown location in April 1972. These cars used Universal brand handbrakes while underneath Keystone 20 inch cushioning systems and Barber S-2-C trucks were applied. Other cars in this series apparently were in general service as they were marked AAR class XM. All cars were rated at either 100 ton capacity or 6,465 cu.ft. *(Paul Winters)*

Insulated Box Car 49546, series 49450-49549

▶ In August 1967, General American manufactured this car. It came equipped with Barber S-2-C trucks, ten foot, six inch Youngstown plug doors and Evans side wall fillers. In addition, an Equipco one piece load divider, Ureco handbrake, Durawood brand hardwood flooring and a Keystone 20 inch cushion system were fitted. Rated at 70 ton capacity or 4,535 cu.ft., this car was found in the Seaboard yard in Birmingham, Alabama in December 1967. It was assigned back to the railroad at Memphis, Tennessee when empty.
(Jim Thorington)

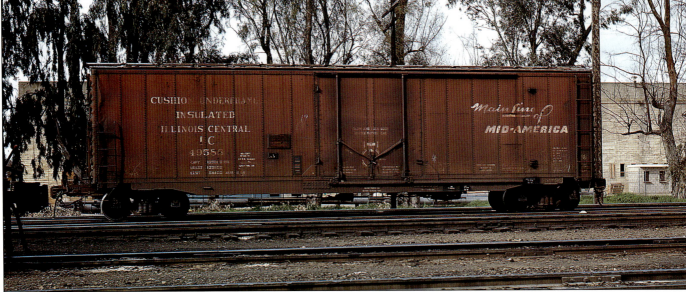

Insulated Box Car 49588, series 49552-49599
▲ The IC's Centralia shops built this RBL car in November 1964. It was fitted with a Keystone 20 inch cushion underframe and had Evans one piece load dividers and six position sidewall fillers along with a Doweloc brand hardwood floor. Barber S-2-C trucks and Youngstown ten foot plug doors were also installed. This group of cars was rated at 70 ton capacity or 4,522 cu.ft. IC 49588 was seen at West Sacramento, California in February 1978. *(Peter Arnold collection)*

Insulated Box Car 49949, series 49900-49965
▼ General American built this group of cars in July 1962 under their Build Order 8270. These cars featured Equipco load dividers and Evans one position sidewall fillers along with Keystone 20 inch cushion underframes. This car, found at an unrecorded location in August 1968, was rated at either 70 ton capacity or 4,638 cu.ft. and had ten foot plug doors along with Barber S-2-C trucks. *(Paul Winters)*

Box Car 117858, series 117800-117999
◀ ACF built this car as part of the original series 17800-17999 in 1938 and 1939. When originally built, these were 40 ton capacity cars but as 50 ton trucks were installed the car numbers were prefixed with the digit "1". Additional cars were built, also by ACF, to make a much larger original number series 17000-18999. This car, still very much in nice IC paint, was spotted in August 1973 at an unrecorded location. It was built in January 1938 and had a capacity of 3,863 cu.ft. Note the yellow stencil indicating the removal of the running boards. *(Bernie Wooller)*

Box Car 119032, series 119000-119299
▲ ACF also built this car, it being manufactured in June 1940. As with the car above, as 50 ton trucks were installed, car numbers were prefixed with the numeral "1". IC 119032, repainted at the McComb shops in March 1964, is shown sitting at Danville Junction, Maine in October 1968. Additional cars were built to this same specification by both ACF (19300-19499) and Mt. Vernon (19500-19999, in two orders) both in 1939 and 1940. These cars were rated at 3,863 cu.ft. *(George Melvin collection)*

Box Car 133275, series 133000-133499
▼ Yet another car with the numeral "1" prefix is this 50'6" inside length box car, found on October 9, 1971 at some unknown location. This car, built in November 1941, came from General American's east Chicago plant. It was originally built as a 40 ton capacity car (although it had been upgraded to a 50 ton car by the time of the photo, as indicated by its new six digit number) and was rated at 4,820 cu.ft. ACF also built similar cars to this same general design in 1941 as original car numbers 33500-33999. *(Peter Arnold collection)*

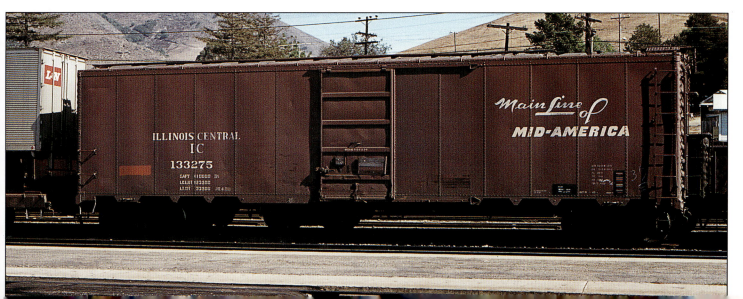

Box Cars in the series 137000-137499

▲▶▼Along with the cars on the prior page, these cars were also renumbered as they acquired 50 ton capacity trucks. Here we get a rare opportunity to observe all three major paint schemes of an interesting 40'6" double door automobile box car. Box car 137078 shows off her *"Main Line of Mid-America"* paint scheme put onto the car at the McComb, Mississippi shops in November 1964. When spotted at Reading, Pennsylvania on October 24, 1970, it was simply assigned "back to the IC RR via the nearest connection" when empty. Built by Mt. Vernon in December 1940, this car shows off its twin seven foot Youngstown doors. Box car 137040 gives us a look at the newer split rail logo in brown Glidden paint applied at Johnson Yard in Memphis, Tennessee in June 1967. Notice that when this car's photo was taken in Huntsville, Alabama in October 1967 the running boards had been removed. It too was built in December 1940. Our final view of these 3,964 cu.ft. cars is the bottom photo, taken in San Luis Obispo, California on November 7, 1971 while in orange paint. Depending on your era of interest and personal preferences you have plenty of paint options to choose from!

(top, Craig Bossler; middle, Bernie Wooller; bottom, Peter Arnold collection)

Box Car 200077, series 200000-200599

▲ In March 1967, the railroad's McComb, Mississippi shops rebuilt IC 200077 from a car out of the 17000-20999 series (built by ACF in 1938 and 1939). These cars basically remained unchanged although this entire series did receive 50 ton trucks and had their running boards removed. A note along the bottom of the car indicates that it received American Marietta paint when rebuilt. This car, found in Broadview, Illinois on October 5, 1978, is in ore service, certainly a rather unusual commodity for a box car. While it appears to have an Ajax handbrake installed, when built new, these cars had either Universal model XL-2000 or Superior handbrakes installed. *(Ray Kucaba)*

Box Car 210101, series 210000-210199

▼ Another rebuilt car is this box car found in Reading, Pennsylvania on September 28, 1973. This car was rebuilt at Johnson Yard in Memphis, Tennessee in August 1967. It comes from the original series 35500-35999 built at Centralia in 1947. Again not much changed during the rebuilding except that all cars received 50 ton trucks and lost their Apex brand running boards. Of course, the new IC split rail emblem was painted onto the car. These cars (both prior to and after the rebuilding) were rated at 3,928 cu.ft. capacity and had twin seven foot Youngstown doors applied along with Klasing handbrakes. *(Craig Bossler)*

Box Car 400666, series 400000-401478

▲ In anticipation of the upcoming IC-GM&O merger, a number of cars from the 22000-23534 series (see page 38) were renumbered into a new six digit series as part of the new numbering plan for the ICG. Here we see one example, found in Huntsville, Alabama in February 1973. These cars, while looking like Pullman-Standard PS-1's, were riveted cars built at Centralia in 1954 and 1955 using some Pullman-Standard parts for their construction. This particular car was repainted at the McComb Shops in May 1972, some three months before the merger. *(Bernie Wooller)*

Box Car 523092, series 523000-523599

▼ Our last Illinois Central box car is this orange car also found in Huntsville, Alabama in February 1973. Like the car above, it too had been renumbered into a new series for the upcoming merger acquiring its paint at Centralia in May 1971. This car originated in the Illinois Central 25000-25899 series (see page 39) built at Centralia in 1956. Other cars from that series were renumbered into numerous other number series' at the time of the merger. *(Bernie Wooller)*

ILLINOIS CENTRAL COVERED HOPPER

Covered Hopper 54208, series 54150-54249
▲ Our first covered hopper is this faded car, seen at Paducah, Kentucky on September 27, 1991, some 31 years after its manufacture by ACF in February 1960. Considering the plain hard work and abuse that these cars received it is amazing that the original paint even has survived all this time. A 70 ton capacity car, it is rated at 2,006 cu.ft. and was in sand service when photographed. For this service, it was assigned to the Burlington at Oregon, Illinois. This group of cars used Keystone outlet gates and was equipped with ASF roller bearing trucks. *(Ray Kucaba)*

Covered Hopper 54448, series 54300-54399
▼ Pullman-Standard's Butler, Pennsylvania plant manufactured this car in October 1961 under their lot 8613. This was followed by covered hoppers 54400-54499, also built by Pullman-Standard in 1961, under lot 8655. These 70 ton capacity cars were built to carry 3,510 cu.ft. of product and used Barber S-2-A trucks and Ellcon National model 1148 handbrakes along with Keystone outlet gates. The photographer found 54448 at Baltimore, Maryland in May, 1985 still very much in original IC paint. *(Jim Rogers)*

Covered Hopper 54898, series 54700-54899

▲ Pullman-Standard's lot 8928 provided this car, built in October 1964 at their Butler, Pennsylvania plant. This 3,510 cu.ft. PS-2 used gravity pneumatic Keystone outlets and ten 30 inch diameter roof hatches. Barber S-2-A trucks were also used. When photographed on July 11, 1995, it was leaving Hagerstown, Maryland in Conrail's NSAL-1, the Norfolk Southern connection (at Hagerstown) to Allentown run. *(Bob Markle)*

Covered Hopper 55430. series 55300-55499

▼ Another 3,510 cu.ft. PS-2 is this car seen at Paducah, Kentucky on September 27, 1991. It is obvious that many Illinois Central covered hoppers kept their original paint well after the coming of the ICG. This car still has its December 1964 new date (!), almost an impossibility for a car nearly 26 years old. Note that the builder's original weights are still stencilled on the cars' side—amazing! These cars were fitted with Ellcon National model 1148 handbrakes, Barber S-2-A trucks and gravity pneumatic Keystone outlets. *(Ray Kucaba)*

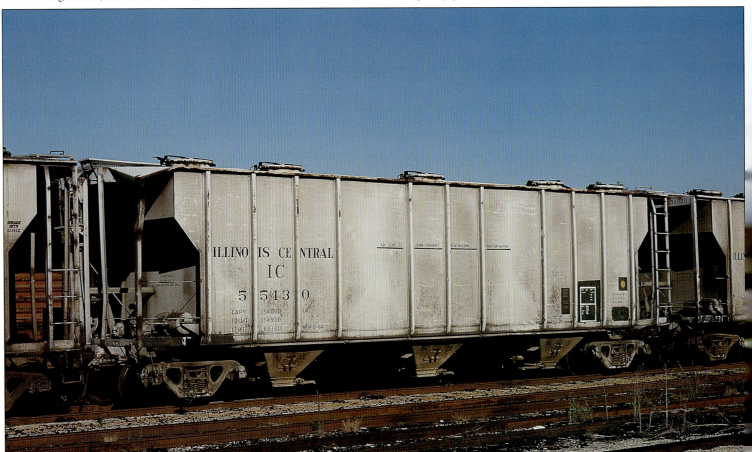

Covered Hopper 56023, series 56000-56299
▲ The railroad's Centralia Shops fabricated this car in October 1966. Built to a 4,740 cu.ft., 100 ton capacity design, these cars used ASF Ride Control trucks, Ellcon National model D-1600-L handbrakes and Keystone outlets. WABCOPAC truck mounted brakes were also fitted. This example was spotted in East St. Louis, Illinois on October 23, 1979. *(Ray Kucaba)*

Covered Hopper 56698, series 56300-56799
▼ Showing its two month old paint, this car was built by General American under lot 8390 in February 1967. Featuring NYCOPAC truck mounted brakes on either Barber S-2-C or, like this car, ASF Ride Control trucks, these cars were rated at either 100 ton capacity or 4,700 cu.ft. Ellcon National D-1600-M handbrakes and Keystone gravity outlets were also utilized. Covered hopper 56698 was found in the Seaboard Air Line yard in Birmingham, Alabama in April 1967. *(Jim Thorington)*

Covered Hopper 56872, series 56800-56899

▲ Repainted in grey, this Pullman-Standard built car was sitting after being loaded with wheat at Wichita, Kansas in December 1989. These cars were rated at either 100 ton capacity or 4,470 cu.ft. (Compare this car's design to the Centralia built car of similar capacity on the prior page.) This group of PS-2CD cars was built in 1969 as Pullman-Standard's lot 9410. They were fitted with Barber S-2-C trucks and Ellcon National D-1600-J handbrakes. The first 30 cars in this series came with Fabko "Roto-Vac" gravity pneumatic outlets but all the rest had Fabko "E-Z Roll" gravity outlets as shown here. *(Jim Kinkaid)*

Covered Hopper 56939, series 56900-57199

▼ The Illinois Central added another 300 cars to their order to Pullman-Standard in 1969 to be produced under lot 9461 in September of that year. One example, in almost new paint, was found in the Seaboard yard at Birmingham, Alabama in April 1970. Like the car above this was a 4,470 cu.ft. PS-2CD and came with Barber S-2-C trucks, however this order used Miner model 6600-L handbrakes and all cars had Fabko "E-Z Roll" gravity outlets. They also utilized four piece fiberglass hatch covers. *(Jim Thorington)*

Airslide 59023, series 59010-59034

▶ Like many railroads, the Illinois Central acquired General American's Airslide covered hoppers for hard to unload products such as flour, sugar and some chemicals. Some cars were purchased directly from the manufacturer (such as the car just below) while others came from the General American lease fleet. Such is the case with this car. Even none-too-close observation will reveal the original GACX reporting marks and predecessor number 43635, from when this car was owned by General American and leased to the IC. When the railroad purchased these cars in 1959, about one year after their manufacture, they repainted them. By the time of this July 1985 photo, taken in Omaha, Nebraska, much of this paint had faded though. These cars employed Barber S-2-A trucks.
(Jim Eager)

Airslide 59156, series 59147-59196

▲ As mention above, the Illinois Central also acquired Airslide cars directly from the builder. One such example is this single bay car found in Muhlenburg Township (one mile north of Reading), Pennsylvania. This 2,600 cu.ft., 70 ton capacity car was built by General American in June 1963. These cars were fitted with Barber S-2-A trucks and Equipco model 3750 handbrakes. *(Craig Bossler)*

Airslide 59263, series 59200-59299

▼ General American also built twin bay Airslide cars for the Illinois Central as witnessed in this view taken at Allentown, Pennsylvania in June 1968. Built in October 1966, it was seen while in Conrail's PIAL-4 train, the Pittsburgh-Allentown run. These cars were rated at either 100 ton capacity or 4,180 cu.ft. Barber S-2-C trucks and Equipco model 4000 handbrakes were used. NYCOPAC truck mounted brakes were also employed. *(Bob Markle)*

Covered Hopper 755365
◀ series 755000-755499

On page 51, we saw the General American series 56300-56799 in grey paint. As these cars were renumbered into a new six digit series for the upcoming ICG merger, some at least received orange paint. This car, spotted in Chicago, Illinois on May 8, 1973, had been repainted at Centralia in March 1972 when it was renumbered. The specifications remained the same as those given for IC 56023 on page 51.

(Dr. Art Peterson)

Covered Hopper 765078, series 765000-765299
▲ By the time these cars were delivered in April 1970, the railroad had begun to assign six digit car numbers in anticipation of the upcoming merger with the GM&O. This changed a long standing practice of assigning five digit car numbers. Here we see one of the newer covered hoppers at West Toronto, Canada while on the Canadian Pacific. This car was built by Pullman-Standard under lot 9489 and was a 4,470 cu.ft. design. This group of cars either had Ellcon National model D-1600-A (first 150 cars) or Ajax (remaining cars) handbrakes while all used Barber S-2-C trucks. Outlets were also split between manufacturers with the first 200 cars receiving Wine gravity outlets and the rest getting a Fabko design.

(Jim Eager)

Covered Hopper 765271, series 765000-765299
▼ Our last view of these Illinois Central covered hoppers is this beautiful shot of brand new PS-2 covered hoppers running down the dual main near Kankakee, Illinois just a few weeks after being built in April 1970. A solid string of these cars on any model layout would certainly look stunning just as the prototypes do here! *(Paul Meyer)*

Flat Car — Illinois Central

Bulkhead Flat Car 60202, series 60200-60299
▲ Our first bulkhead flat car is this Centralia built car found sitting in Ft. Dodge, Iowa (where it was assigned to) on August 7, 1984. These cars were assembled over General Steel Industries one piece cast underframes, easily noted by their multi-taper drop side sills. Built in 1960, this group of cars had their bulkheads extended two feet in 1967 as can be seen clearly in this end view. ASF Ride Control trucks were installed as was an Ajax handbrake. Assigned to wallboard service, these cars had lading strap anchors welded near the side stake pockets. Note the white paint on the outer sides of the stake pockets. *(Peter Arnold)*

Bulkhead Flat Car 60469, series 60300-60470
▼ Built by Bethlehem Steel Company in July 1963, this car was part of an overall series 60300-60499. The first 471 cars (including this car) were plainly equipped while the additional cars in the number series 60471-60499 had eleven tie down chains with load binders, corner guards and lading skids for packaged lumber. It is interesting to note that this car has twin markings on the bulkheads: the upper line represents the maximum load height for gypsum board while the lower line is the maximum height for hardboard. All cars came equipped with Barber S-2-A trucks. This car appeared to have had a Universal brand handbrake installed when found in Huntsville, Alabama at an unknown date. *(Bernie Wooller)*

Bulkhead Flat Car 61566, series 61500-61699

▲ This 61 foot inside length bulkhead flat car was sitting in Chicago, Illinois waiting for repairs when found on April 28, 1985. Built by the Evans Company in 1967 under lot 1-5001, these cars were equipped with chain bins (along the lower sills) and 18 tie down ratchet assemblies. When new, they also had corner guards and lading skids for packaged lumber service though no doubt these items have long disappeared. Barber S-2-A trucks and Universal model 7400 handbrakes were installed on the cars as were NYCOPAC truck-mounted brakes. *(Ray Kucaba)*

Flat Car 62119, series 62100-62474

▼ The Illinois Central's Centralia Shops built this car in April 1950 some 36 years before its photo was taken on April 28, 1985. While obviously having seen better days, this flat car was still going strong when found sitting in a Chicago, Illinois rail yard. These cars were 53'6" long over end sills and were rated at 50 ton capacity. *(Ray Kucaba)*

Heavy Duty Flat Car 62499, series 62499

▲ Considering the major industrial areas such as Chicago and New Orleans that the Illinois Central served it is a bit surprising that the railroad didn't own more "exotic" flat cars than it did. One such heavy duty flat is this six axle car seen at some unknown location in August 1964. Built at Centralia in April 1953 from a General Steel Industries cast flat car, this was a 125 ton capacity car. From the looks of this multi-car load it is obviously receiving a workout on this trip! Universal model 2110 dual handbrakes were utilized, one on each end of this massive car. This car as not as long as it appeared however, being only 53'0" long over end sills. *(Paul Winters)*

Flat Car 62630, series 62625-62674

▼ Another General Steel cast flat is this example found at College Park, Missouri in April 1970 hauling several cement mixer tanks. It was built at Centralia in 1962. These 60'0" long cars were part of a continuing order comprising a total number series 62600-62674, dating back to 1957. ASF Ride Control trucks were installed on these cars. Note the small hole in the side sill to right of the car's number: this was for the adjusting shaft for the Universal brand rotary slack adjuster, a common device prior to automatic slack adjusters installed in later years. *(Jim Rogers)*

Flat Car 62811, series 62725-62824

▲ Still in nice as-built American Marietta paint when found on Chesapeake and Ohio rails in Columbus, Ohio in June 1972, this flat was hauling a Caterpillar dirt scraper. Built by the Centralia Shops in November 1965, it was assigned to the Peoria and Pekin Union Railroad at Peoria, Illinois. This group of cars was equipped with ASF Ride Control trucks and Universal model 5934 drop shaft handbrakes. They had decks 60' 1/2" long over end sills. *(Dick Argo)*

Bulkhead Flat Car 920487, series 920400-920599

▼ On page 55, we showed bulkhead flat 60469 in original paint. Here, one of the cars from that series has been repainted and renumbered into a six digit number for the impending merger. This bulkhead flat was seen at Mason City, Iowa on May 30, 1980 waiting on another load. The specifications for this 48' 6" inside length car are the same as for IC 60469. *(Peter Arnold)*

Coil Car 941036, series 941025-941049

▲ The United States Railway Equipment Company built these exotic cars in May 1971 under lot 819-B. Designed to handle coiled steel, these cars were rated at 100 ton and had dual troughs under each of the 23'4" removable roofs. This car was only two months old when spotted in Council Bluffs, Iowa on July 18, 1971. Assigned back to the IC's Markham Yard in Chicago when empty it had Barber S-2-A trucks and a 20 inch Hydra Cushion underframe. *(Lou Schmitz)*

Centerbeam Flat Car 945084, series 945000-945099

▼ Certainly one of the more unusual cars on the railroad were these "A" frame (also known as centerbeam) flat cars built by Centralia in November 1970. Designed exclusively for packaged lumber, these cars had a 61' 1/8" inside length. Ajax handrakes and Barber S-2-C trucks were installed. To help secure the lumber loads, 34 tie down chain assemblies, along with 34 corner guards and lading strap anchors were provided. These very interesting cars would make for an eye catching model on any post 1970 era layout. This example was spotted in Huntsville, Alabama in September 1971. *(Bernie Wooller)*

ILLINOIS CENTRAL GONDOLA

Gondola 2355, series 2300-2399
▶ Converted at the McComb, Mississippi shops in 1962 for log service, this open-sided gondola was in raw tie service when spotted in Paducah, Kentucky on September 20, 1987. This group of cars had been converted at random from cars out of the 94000-95499 drop bottom gondola class, those cars having been built at Centralia in 1953. Although the drop doors have been permanently closed for this log/tie service, note that the operating shafts and chains are still installed. These were 50 ton capacity, 1,947 cu.ft. 41'0" inside length gondolas.
(Ray Kucaba)

Gondola 85725, series 85000-85999
▲ A much more pristine drop bottom gondola is this car built by the railroad in July 1952. This car was a 50 ton capacity car rated at 1,947 cu.ft., all of which (and probably more) was in use this rainy day hauling coal. This group of cars was furnished with ASF A-3 or Scullin S-2 trucks and either Ajax or Miner handbrakes. Standard Railway furnished the drop doors on these 41'0" inside length cars. The date and location of this photograph is unknown but likely dates from the mid 1950's. *(Emery Gulash)*

Gondola 96891, series 96000-96929
▼ By the time of this photo, taken in Binghamton, New York in March 1969, the Illinois Central had permanently closed off most, if not all, of the drop bottom doors on their classic 41' gondolas. This car shows how even the door shafts and chains have been removed. These cars were converted from the drop bottom gondola series 94000-95499 built by the railroad's Centralia Shops in 1953, this car having been built in June of that year.
(Bill Folsom)

Gondola 97379, series 97350-97499

▶ Although the paint has gotten pretty scruffy, it hasn't affected its load carrying abilities any! Shown here with an oversized box beam load in Jessup, Maryland in August 1989, this car was built by Bethlehem Steel in March 1966. A 65'6" inside length mill gon, it has a steel floor (although it did have timber posts and floor crossbeams when new), Barber S-2-A trucks and an Ellcon National model D-1802 handbrake. "Tu Way" lading band anchors are barely visible along the cars top chord. Rated at 100 ton capacity, it will also haul 3,243 cu.ft. *(Jim Rogers)*

Covered Gondola 99832, series 99800-99894

▲ Covered gondolas are always interesting to look at, and this Centralia built example is no exception. Built in December 1964 and assigned back to the IC at Birmingham, Alabama when empty, it was found far from home at San Luis Obispo, California on November 24, 1979. Outside, ASF Ride Control trucks and a Universal model 2250 handbrake was fitted along with a three-piece removable roof. Inside, besides the wood floor, the car had four movable bulkheads and four belt rails, all to better secure the structural steel that this car hauled. This series was rated at 70 ton capacity or 2,245 cu.ft. IC 99832 will likely be snagged for repairs soon: note that torn up running board on the near end. *(Peter Arnold)*

Gondola 99949, series 99900-99949

▼ The last car in this series, Illinois Central 99949 sits with a load of tubular steel in Cicero, Illinois on December 23, 1977. Built by Bethlehem Steel under lot 348 in November 1964, this classic 65'6" inside length mill gon is rated at either 70 ton capacity or 1,799 cu.ft. These cars used Barber S-2-A trucks and Universal model 1995 lever handbrakes. *(Ray Kucaba)*

Covered Gondola 295506, series 295500-295549
▲ Oh well...not every car in a freight train can be pristine. This gondola, having seen better days with its paint, sits in Forest View, Illinois on New Years Day 1993. It was built by Greenville Steel in 1967 under lot 925. A three piece Republic removable roof is installed, and it needs some attention to detail, just as does the paint. This group of cars used Barber S-2-C trucks and Ellcon National handbrakes. Cushioning for these cars were 20 inch Keystone units. These cars were clean inside (so to speak), lacking any belt rails or load dividers. *(Ray Kucaba)*

Gondola 296005, series 296000-296099
▼ Another case of renumbering cars to better fit a master Illinois Central Gulf number plan for the post merger is this series of solid bottom gondolas. These cars were taken from the series 94000-95499 built by Centralia in 1953 as drop bottom gondolas. This original series of cars provided many renumberings over the years and several are illustrated elsewhere in this Color Guide. This example was found sitting in Reading, Pennsylvania on September 20, 1970. Note the lack of any reweigh date. *(Craig Bossler)*

INTERMODAL — ILLINOIS CENTRAL

IC vans

▲▼ In the upper view, IC trailers T-40111 and T-40154 are loaded onto TTX 300012, a rather rare General American G-85 flat car, built under build order 8219 in May 1961. Seen at Homewood, Illinois in December 1963, these 85' cars would be shortly superseded by longer 87' and 89 foot flats. The inside post van is part of the IC series T-40100-40124 and was rated at 2,392 cu.ft. The outside post van is part of the series T-40150-40199 and was rated at 2,446 cu.ft. Both were 39 foot dry van trailers. In the lower view, recorded at Council Bluffs, Iowa on May 4, 1969, are two newly built 2,020 cu.ft. vans from the ICZ series 501200-501299. These were refrigerated 39 foot inside length trailers equipped with both Thermo-King nose mounted refrigeration packages and meat rails (with the insulation and rails no doubt contributing to the lower cubical capacity than the vans above). TTX 154925, carrying the ICZ vans, was built in March 1967 by Bethlehem Steel under lot 3400-048 and TTX-classed F89e. Note that it has a newer style Trailer Train paint scheme than the car above. Duplicating either car/trailer set on any model railroad would make for a sure standout in any train! *(top, Emery Gulash; bottom Lou Schmitz)*

Flexi Van 911, series 903-925
▶ Along with several other roads the Illinois Central was a user of Flexi Van service. These cars were especially valuable due to the amount of head end mail business that the railroad moved. The IC had two versions of these cars. IC 900-902 were the earlier Flexi Van cars, probably acquired secondhand from the NYC (under MFVX reporting marks) in December 1959. IC 903-925 cars were the later Mk IV designs built by Greenville Steel Car under two orders: Office Order 846 (for 14 cars) and Office Order 879A (for the remaining nine). Unfortunately, between the U.S. Mail being removed from the railroads and the rise of more conventional methods of container carriage, these cars became less and less necessary. IC 911 sits in South Modena, Pennsylvania on November 10, 1973, awaiting its turn with the torch.
(Craig Bossler)

Autorack, RTTX 250175
▲ Like most railroads, the Illinois Central used Trailer Train for flat car equipment onto which the road added their own racks. One such example sits at an unknown location in May 1967. Like most equipment of this type these cars were in a pool service and sometimes never even ran on their own rails. This car, for example, was assigned to the Union Pacific at Kansas City, Missouri. The flat car, a TTX class F89e standard deck car, was built by Pullman-Standard in August 1963 under lot 8819-D while the rack is a Whitehead and Kales fixed deck, cushioned trilevel. The rack was cushioned because the car wasn't. *(Paul Winters)*

Autorack, KTTX 904351
▼ A more modern car is this partially enclosed tri level autorack found in February 1974 transporting a load of Ford Pintos. As vandalism became more and more of a problem, the railroads attempted to limit their losses by installing rock shields on the sides of the cars. Eventually this type of car had to go to a fully enclosed design. This Trailer Train class F89ch low level flat was built by Pullman-Standard under lot 9139-C in June 1966 and has a Whitehead and Kales Lo-Tri-Pak hinged-end rack installed.
(Paul Winters)

REFRIGERTOR ILLINOIS CENTRAL

Refrigerator NRC 16609, series 16500-16799

▼ The Illinois Central was a prime mover of bananas and other perishable fruits from the ports of New Orleans. While the road owned its own fleet of refrigerator cars, they also leased equipment from the NRC. This DSI built car was spotted at the Southern's 42nd Street crossing in Birmingham, Alabama in March 1969 near the end of ice operations. It received the split rail logo at New Orleans in March 1968 when it was repainted. This car was part of a series built in 1953 and 1954 under DSI's lot 891. These cars were added to a similar group of cars built in 1952 under lot 881 making for an overall car number series 16000-16799. *(Jim Thorington)*

Refrigerator NRC 19414, series 19400-19499

▲ This rather unusual refrigerator car sits in the Norfolk and Western's Joyce Avenue Yard in Columbus, Ohio in November 1962. It had just been repainted when photographed and has what appears to be flat ends, probably replacements installed during some repairs. This refrigerator car was part of the series of cars built by Despatch Shops in 1950 under lot 892. Like almost all of this equipment, it was assigned back to the IC at New Orleans when empty. *(Paul Winters)*

Refrigerator 58212, series 58200-58224

▼ This Illinois Central marked car was caught sitting at Council Bluffs, Iowa on June 14, 1964. The series that this car came from was renumbered from the original IC series 50000-50299 built by General American at their East Chicago, Indiana plant in 1937 under their Build Order 2782. This group of cars had Equipco sectional ice bunkers installed and their Preco fans removed. Ajax handbrakes were installed on these cars as were Hutchins roofs.

(Lou Schmitz)

ILLINOIS CENTRAL HOPPER

**Hopper 66221
series 65300-66699**

▶ Hopewell, Virginia was the location of this Centralia-built open hopper in June 1966. This triple hopper was built in August 1965 and was rated at 70 ton capacity or 3,263 cu.ft. at level full. These cars were 40'8" inside length and a mixture of ASF and Barber trucks were utilized. Enterprise Unit-Latch door locks were also used.
(Dr. Art Peterson)

Hopper 68911, series 68000-68999

▲ Built in September 1937, this twin hopper was still hauling the goods when located at some unrecorded location in May 1966. This car was from a series that had been renumbered at random from the original 209000-209999. These cars were fabricated by Ryan-Hegewisch and were rated at 50 ton capacity or 2,145 cu.ft. The cars were fitted with Ajax handbrakes and a variety of truck designs. *(Bob Wilt)*

Hopper 69454, series 69000-69999

▼ Another group of cars renumbered at random from an earlier number series is represented by this clean car, found at some unrecorded location on August 21, 1960, four months to the day since it had its air brake tested after having been repainted at Centralia. When built new by General American in September 1937, it belonged to the IC number series 219000-219999. A standard 33'0" inside length twin hopper, it has a Universal brand handbrake installed, although like the hopper shown just above, numerous truck designs were utilized. *(Bill Folsom)*

Hopper 73216, series 73000-73599

▶ Nearing the end of its useful life, this rebuilt war emergency hopper was spotted in October 1966 at some unknown location. When originally built by the railroad in 1944, these cars had a cubical capacity of 1,970 cu.ft. After the Illinois Central rebuilt these 50 ton capacity cars in 1955 by replacing the wood sides and slope sheets with steel sheets, the capacity was increased to 2,045 cu.ft. Wine door locks were installed and the handbrakes were evenly split between Universal brand and Ajax. *(Bob Wilt)*

Hoppers 82067 and 83150, series 82000-83499

▲▼ Here are two views of hopper cars from the same class although taken some 15 years apart. At (center) these consecutively numbered hoppers have just been loaded at the Peabody Coal Company's Freeburg, Illinois plant on August 28, 1960, two months after having been built. In a couple of years (1962 and 1963) these two cars would receive 16 inch side and end extensions raising their cubical capacity from an as-built 2,773 cu.ft. to 3,290 cu.ft. They would become part of the 82000-82234 group of similarly modified cars with the remaining cars not being so modified. ASF trucks were installed as were Keystone Monoloc door locks on these 70 ton capacity cars. The bottom photo, taken in Chicago in October 1975, gives us an excellent peek into the interior of one of these cars. This car was from the unmodified group of cars in the series 82235-83499. ASF A-3 trucks were installed on hoppers 82235-82999 while Barber S-2-A trucks went under 83000-83499. *(above, Bill Folsom; bottom, Dr. Art Peterson)*

Hopper 78922, series 78000-78999

▲ Although a considerably newer car than the one on the previous page, this quadruple open hopper's paint is pretty rough due to the hard service it has encountered. Built by the Centralia Shops in September 1968, this car was spotted far from home hauling coal at San Luis Obispo, California on July 16, 1980. These cars were rather large for coal cars, at 3,834 cu.ft., and were rated at 100 ton capacity. Barber S-2-C trucks along with Keystone Monoloc door locks were installed. Large numbers of similar cars were built by Centralia for Inland Steel Company service with some 2,420 additional cars being built through 1977.

(Peter Arnold)

Caboose 8009, series 8000-8020

▼ The Illinois Central rebuilt a number of box cars from the 10000 series into terminal cabooses. This example was assigned to New Orleans and was photographed at—where else?—New Orleans in April 1967. This caboose was rebuilt in 1948, although the rebuilds continued on through 1951. These cars had coal stoves installed along with Ajax handbrakes.

(Arthur Angstadt photo, Hawk Mountain Chapter, NRHS)

Caboose 8095, series 8091-8115
▲ The Illinois Central terminal caboose cars converted from the 10000 series box cars (in 1951) resulted in an overall IC number series 8000-8115. They were built in four groups (actually six if one includes the Chicago and Illinois Western subsidiary cabooses built in two batches of two each in 1949 and 1953-54 and numbered CI&W 3 through 6). Crossing the diamonds in Chicago, Illinois in October 1969 terminal caboose 8095 is from the last of these conversions having been rebuilt in 1951. Note the elliptic springs in the trucks. *(Dr. Art Peterson)*

Caboose 9403, series 9400-9449
▼ The Centralia shops built these car in 1971. In 1972, an additional 50 cars were also manufactured and placed in the 9350-9399 number series. All these cars used Barber swing motion trucks (easily noted by the elliptic springs) and Ajax handbrakes. A twelve volt lighting system was installed along with an oil heater. In addition, this series was cushioned with a Keystone system. This example was found on the roll at Broadview, Illinois on a cold November 28, 1977. *(Ray Kucaba)*

Caboose 9534, series 9500-9549
▲ A friendly wave greets the photographer in this view taken in Chicago, Illinois in October 1969. Built by the Darby Corporation in 1968, this car was equipped with an oil heater and twelve volt electrical system driven from the axle (note the drive shaft extending from the left hand truck). Barber swing motion trucks and Keystone 20 inch cushioning systems were also employed on these cars along with URECO handbrakes. *(Dr. Art Peterson)*

Caboose 9592, series 9550-9599
▼ Scooting along in Chicago, Illinois, this caboose was photographed on May 1, 1971. It was part of a series of cars built at the railroad's Centralia shops in 1969. Like the car above, Barber swing motion trucks, a Keystone 20 inch cushion system, twelve volt axle driven electrical system and oil heater was installed however these cars were fitted with Miner handbrakes. *(Dr. Art Peterson)*

Caboose 9789, series 9701-9799
▶ Built in October 1940, this freshly painted caboose sits in Markam Yard on October 27, 1957. Built at Centralia, this car was actually part of a much larger series than the heading indicates. In 1939, Centralia built caboose 9700 and again in 1941 they outfitted even more cars in the series 9800-9899. Ajax handbrakes were used while various second hand trucks were utilized. *(W.A. Gibson photo, W. Woelfer collection)*

Caboose 9771, series 9701-9799
◀ I just had to include this excellent shot of one of these side door cabooses in action. On July 22, 1962, orders were being picked up on the fly at Gilman, Illinois for this Springfield bound freight. That side door obviously made catching those orders on the run much easier. *(Melvern Finzer)*

Caboose 9903, series 9900-9949
▼ On February 2, 1963, caboose 9903 was found sitting in Council Bluffs, Iowa. It was built by the railroad in December 1950 and used Ajax handbrakes. While most of the cars in this series used side doors, caboose cars 9900-9917 had these omitted due to an Iowa law that did not allow the use of side door equipped cabooses. *(Lou Schmitz)*

Caboose 9907, series 9900-9949
► Another car from the series built in 1950 is this one in split rail paint. It was found in Chicago, Illinois in November 1971. Note that it too lacks the side doors so common on older IC cabooses.
(Howard Robins)

**Cabooses 9925 & 9649,
series 9900-9949 and 9600-9649**
▼ A couple of classic IC side door caboose cars sits at Ft. Knox, Kentucky in October 1962. Caboose 9925 is from the same series as the car above and on the prior page. Note, of course, that side doors have been installed on this car. Caboose 9649 is from a 50 car series built by the railroad in 1957 and 1958. These cars had Barber swing motion trucks and Ajax handbrakes. Keystone hydraulic end of car cushioning was installed. *(Dick Argo)*

**Caboose 9985
series 9950-9999**
◄ Our last caboose is this side door car found sitting in Council Bluffs, Iowa on May 15, 1954. These cars were built by the railroad in 1951 and were added to the earlier series 9900-9949, shown on this page and the prior page. It is hard to believe that the paint could have faded so badly in only three years. As with the earlier series, some cars in this group also had their side doors omitted. Those cars had the numbers 9950-9967. Like the earlier group, this series also had Ajax brakes and swing motion trucks.
(Lou Schmitz)

MAINTENANCE OF WAY — ILLINOIS CENTRAL

Safety Instruction Car 12
▶ This safety instruction car was found sitting in Chicago, Illinois on March 2, 1969 about six months before it was sold in August. Assigned to the personnel department, it originated as 88 seat coach car 2284. Part of the coach series 2280-2286, it was built by Pullman in 1925 under lot 4858. *(Owen Leander)*

Safety Special Car 14
◀ Converted from salon-buffet 4065, safety special car 14 sits in Cedar Rapids, Iowa in October 1971. Built by Pullman in 1924 under lot 4735, this car was apparently converted to maintenance of way service in late 1967 or early 1968. As built, it featured a 12 place dining room and a 21 seat salon along with wrap around couches at both ends of the car. A small kitchen and pantry were also installed. Just what interior modifications were involved with this "service with safety" car is unknown.
(Ron Plazzotta)

Technical Instruction Car 15
▶ Repainted in a split rail MofW orange paint scheme, ex-observation 3310 (named *Mark Beaubien*) sits in Chicago on July 12, 1969. This observation was a multiple conversion car like some of the other observation cars that the railroad owned. It originated as coach 2189 out of the coach series 2168-2206. (For views of several of these observation cars in "real" Illinois Central paint, see page 15.) It was once again converted in 1968 after having been retired in 1967 and placed into maintenance of way service. A 24 seat training area was installed with a black board and movie screen dividing the seating area from the observation area where five lounge seats were installed. A small six seat office and projector room completed the modification. *(Owen Leander)*

Locomotive Service Car X553
▲ This interesting car was found in Fulton, Kentucky on March 9, 1981. For those modelling the diesel era, this diesel fuel and sand tender conversion might be just the model to attempt! *(Steve Johnson)*

Diesel Fuel Car X753
▼ As if it wasn't bad enough for a once mighty steam locomotive tender to be downgraded to diesel fuel status, the railroad went and installed a tank car dome and platform on the top! This modified tender was spotted at Homewood, Illinois on March 14, 1970. *(Owen Leander)*

MofW Flat X2885
▶ Here is a very unusual flat car conversion. Running over old E unit three axle trucks, it was used to move locomotive wheel sets from the 27th Street yard to the Markham Roundhouse. This flat car was found in Chicago, Illinois on May 13, 1967.
(Owen Leander)

Scale Car X8004
◀ A common item found around many rail yards is a scale car. Used to confirm proper operation of track scales, there were many variants on the idea, but the scale cars manufactured by Atlas were very common. One such example sits in the snow at Council Bluffs, Iowa on January 30, 1955. It was built in May 1925. *(Lou Schmitz)*

Rail Detector Car RDC1
▼ This unusual piece of maintenance of way rolling stock was found sitting on a siding in Clinton, Illinois in May 1973. While rail detection equipment normally invoked the image of the Sperry Company's rail detector cars, the Illinois Central also performed this operation. Note those classic marker lamps front and rear!
(Russ Porter)

Derrick X101
▲ Like any major railroad the Illinois Central kept a number of cranes and derricks on hand for both routine and not so routine operations found along the line. This immaculate steam powered derrick was spotted in Carbondale, Illinois on May 31, 1958.
(Lou Schmitz)

Plow X8012
▼ With the severe snow storms that the Illinois Central often found itself in the midst of in the Midwestern states, snow plows were essential equipment. One was kept at Ft. Dodge, Iowa for just such a storm. This Russell plow was found there on March 27, 1954. Although there isn't any snow to be seen on the date of this photo, the possibilities of a late season blizzard certainly mandated keeping the plow in a "ready to go" condition! *(Lou Schmitz)*

GM&O PASSENGER

Baggage-Mail 32, series 29-33

▶ Baggage-mail 32 travels within Chicago, Illinois in June 1967. This series comprised various cars built by ACF, Pullman and Bethlehem Steel in the 1920's. Car 32 was built by ACF's Jeffersonville plant in June 1927 under lot 413 for the Mobile and Ohio, and in 1940 modified and streamlined for GULF COAST REBEL service between East St. Louis and Mobile, Alabama, which was inaugurated on October 29, 1940. The modifications included a streamline roof and skirting. This car would be retired on November 10, 1971 and sold to D.J. Joseph in Beech Grove, Indiana. *(Ron Plazzotta)*

RPO 45, series 45-46

▲ Unlike the two cars featured above, this RPO remains in its as built condition. RPO 45 was originally built by Pullman for the Chicago and Alton in 1930 as number 909. It became the Alton's 65 and then the GM&O's 45. This RPO was spotted working its way past a St. Louis interlocking in March 1967. *(Ron Plazzotta)*

RPO 41, series 40-42

▼ This freshly repainted Railway Post Office car was found traversing the slip switches in St. Louis in September 1967. This RPO was one of three built of Harriman design for the Chicago and Alton in 1914 by Pullman under lot 4283 as C&A 904-906. This car, ex-C&A 905, would later become Alton 61 and then be renumbered GM&O 41. *(Paul Winters)*

Baggage-Express 64, series 62-67
▲ In January 1927, the Mobile and Ohio ordered six baggage-express cars from ACF to be delivered as numbers 62-67. They were produced at ACF's Jeffersonville, Indiana plant in June 1927 under lot 412. Car 64's number conflicted with a similar car already built by Pullman in 1926 so 64 was renumbered by the M&O to 64M. Renumbered (again) by the GM&O as simply 64 (the original Pullman built 64 was renumbered by the GM&O to 69) it was found in Chicago, Illinois in February 1968. This baggage-express car would be condemned on November 10, 1971.
(Ron Plazzotta)

Baggage-Express 91, series 90-91, 164
▼ This baggage car was one of three built for the Gulf, Mobile and Northern by ACF's Jeffersonville plant under lot 577 in April 1928. Originally numbered GM&N 63 and subsequently renumbered 38, it was rebuilt in November 1952. Note the blanked off door and window locations on the near end of the car which probably occurred during the rebuilding. Shown leaving Chicago's Union Station in July 1966, this car would be condemned in December 1969.
(Ron Plazzotta)

Baggage 93, series 92-93
▶ In 1928, Pullman built this car for the Chicago and Alton as that road's number 54 under lot 6189. It was rebuilt in December 1952. In April 1967, baggage 93 was found working its way though the extensive trackage in Chicago in company with numerous other head end cars. Like baggage-express 64 pictured at the top of this page, this car would also be condemned on November 10, 1971.
(Ron Plazzotta)

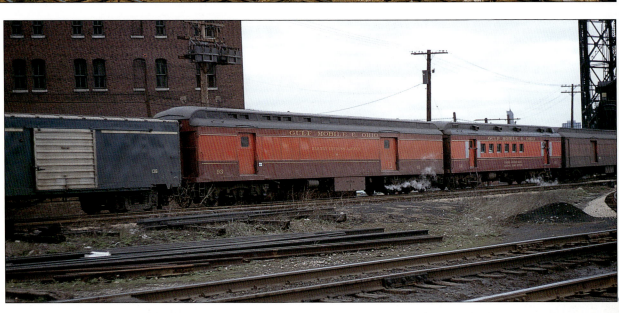

Baggage 400, series 400-419

▶ Although this Pullman built series was listed in the *Official Register of Passenger Train Equipment* issues as running from 400-419, three different configurations were used to create this series. The cars were originally built in 1910, 1911, 1913 (as this car was) and 1916 as club cars. Baggage 400 was originally built as the *Barnegat* under lot 4158 and was rebuilt to this configuration in 1941. In June 1967, it was spotted in Chicago, Illinois. Baggage 400 would wind up being sold to D.J. Joseph in Beech Grove, Indiana.
(Ron Plazzotta)

Baggage 451, series 450-464

▲ As the Delaware and Hudson's baggage cars in their 401-425 series became unneeded in the early 1960's, 15 were purchased by the GM&O. Though never repainted into the GM&O's red and maroon (plus black roof, underframe and trucks) scheme, they did received new numbers. Built by ACF in 1957 (under lot 04-4947) as the D&H's 423, and rebuilt in 1962, baggage 451 is in Chicago, Illinois in July 1963. Because of their relative newness compared to the GM&O's other baggage cars, a number of these lightweight baggage cars were transferred to ICG maintenance of way service. *(Paul Winters)*

Combine 2592, series 2592

▼ This combine originated as the Chicago and Alton's 675, the *Jefferson* (a parlor car), built by Pullman in 1924. Built for the ALTON LIMITED it was renumbered to Alton 1487. By the time it was spotted in Chicago, Illinois in May 1967, this car had undergone several prior modifications. Sometime before 1943 it had been rebuilt as a passenger-baggage car seating 36 and incorporating a 39 foot baggage area. Then, between late 1947 and early 1949 it was rebuilt again as a 34 seat, 33 foot baggage car, primarily for ABRAHAM LINCOLN service. In a little over two years after this photo (September 1969), it would be stricken from the GM&O's roster. *(Ron Plazzotta)*

Combine 2594, series 2594
▶ Combine 2594 was built for the Chicago and Alton for ALTON LIMITED service by Pullman in 1924 as the *Missouri*. It was numbered by the C&A as combine 713 and renumbered by the Alton to 1489. In the late 1940's or early 1950's, it became the GM&O's 2594 with the baggage area reduced from 36 feet to 25 feet. Combine 2594 was found approaching Chicago's Union Station on March 22, 1969. *(Owen Leander)*

Coach 141, series 140-141
▲ Built by ACF in June 1927 under lot 408 for the Gulf, Mobile and Northern (with the same numbers), one of these 62 seat coaches was found in Chicago-Joliet suburban service leaving Chicago, Illinois on May 16, 1971. *(Owen Leander)*

Coach 209, series 209-210
▼ Coach 209 sits in Chicago, Illinois on August 29, 1971. These two cars have kept their original Mobile and Ohio numbers through the years. Ordered in December 1925 and built by ACF in July 1926 under lot 140 at Jeffersonville, Indiana, these cars seated 62 patrons. Although part of the overall series 209-216, this larger series incorporated similar cars built by Pullman and Bethlehem Steel. This coach was slated for retirement in September 1969. *(Owen Leander)*

Coach-Lounge 243, series 242-243
▲ The Gulf, Mobile and Northern was the original owner of this coach-lounge car, as their 143. Built by ACF in 1928 under lot 576, it had coach seating for 44 and with another four in the midship lounge. It was noteworthy in that it was the only ex GM&N car modified (in October 1940) and placed in GULF COAST REBEL service. When rebuilt for GULF COAST REBEL service, it was designated a coach-dorm with six berths in the dormitory area. Sister 242, ex GM&N 142, was a regular coach which seated 72 and kept its clerestory roof. Coach 243 was in Chicago to Joilet commuter service when spotted in August 1970. It would be stricken from the roster on August 23, 1972. *(Ron Plazzotta)*

Coach 244, series 244-245
▼ Coach 244 was built by Pullman in 1924 for the Chicago and Alton's ALTON LIMITED and named *Lincoln*. A 34 seat parlor car, it was renumbered by the Alton to 2102, prior to the GM&O's further renumbering to 244. This 96 seat coach, modified from parlor to coach, is seen in Chicago in August 1970 coupled to coach-lounge 243 (shown above). *(Ron Plazzotta)*

Coach 2207, series 2207
▶ Coach 2207 sits in Chicago, Illinois on June 29, 1969 just four months prior to being stricken from the roster in September 1969. At this time it was a 40 seat car. Prior to its conversion and renumbering in July 1961, it was a ten section, one drawing room, two compartment sleeper named *Lake Selby*, originally built by Pullman under lot 4898 in August 1925 for Pullman service. When rebuilt for coach service, the bulkheads between the sections were removed and coach seats installed.
(Owen Leander)

Coach 3051, series 3050-3060
▲ A 68 seat coach, this car was seen in Chicago. Illinois on May 16, 1971. It was built by ACF under lot 2882 at St. Charles, Missouri and was part of a series of eleven coaches delivered by that firm in November and December 1947 for Chicago to St. Louis service. While considered a lightweight car by the road, note that it had six wheel trucks for better riding qualities. *(Owen Leander)*

Coach 3099, series 3096-3099
▼ This 84 seat coach was originally built by Pullman in 1924 for the Chicago and Alton. Used on the ALTON LIMITED as a chair car, it was named *Oak Park*. By the time of its photographing in Chicago Illinois in May 1967, four seats had been removed. *(Ron Plazzotta)*

Coach 5801, series 5801-5802
▶ This 64 seat aluminum coach was part of an eight-car trainset built by ACF in May 1935 for the B&O's ROYAL BLUE service. In April 1937, the consist (including this car) was transferred to the Alton for ABRAHAM LINCOLN Chicago to St. Louis service. Here it is seen outside Chicago's Union Station in May 1967. In September 1969, it would be stricken from the GM&O's roster.
(Ron Plazzotta)

Coach 5804, series 5804-5805

▶ Of similar configuration (64 seats) to the car described on the bottom of the previous page, this Cor-Ten steel coach was also built by ACF in May 1935. In July 1935, it (along with the rest of the steel eight car trainset) was placed in the Alton's ABRAHAM LINCOLN service. On July 26, 1937, when the aluminum cars were transferred to this run, these cars were then moved over to ANN RUTLEDGE service. Here it is seen at St. Louis in May 1967. It would be sent into retirement on September 29, 1969.

(Ron Plazzotta)

Diner 1075, series 1075-1076

◀ This port hole equipped, 40 seat diner was found in St. Louis in September 1967. It was originally built by Pullman in August 1930 (as lot 6386) as a parlor car for the B&O's COLUMBIAN service and named the *Lincoln Memorial*. It would then be sold to the Alton on June 22, 1944 and eventually be renumbered to GM&O 2104 (the second). In 1949, the GM&O's Bloomington Shops rebuilt this car from a straight parlor car to a diner. Mate 1076 originated as the Alton's parlor car 2106, which was originally Chicago and Alton 673, the *Cleveland*.

(Paul Winters)

Diner-Lounge 2008-*Azalea*, series 2008

▶ On May 2, 1967, this diner-lounge was also found in St. Louis. Originally the Chicago and Alton's 663, *Azalea* was built by Pullman in 1925 under lot 4958 and rebuilt in 1948. It seated 24 passengers in the dining area and another 20 in the lounge. After its 1948 rebuilding this car was used in *Gulf Coast Rebel* service until that train was discontinued on October 14, 1958.

(Arthur Angstadt, Hawk Mountain Chapter, NRHS)

Diner 5700, series 5700
▶ Found in Chicago in May 1967, this was originally a diner-lunch counter car that was part of the aluminum eight car trainset built by ACF for the B&O's Royal Blue service. Along with the other cars, it was moved to the Alton's trains 18 and 19, the Ann Rutledge, in 1937. In 1946, it was rebuilt to a 40 seat dining car. The rebuilding consisted of removing the lunch counter from one end and moving the kitchen from the center of the car to the lounge end. This car was retired in September 1969.
(Ron Plazzotta)

Parlor-*Springfield*, series 2106-2109
◀ *Springfield* was one of four parlor cars built by ACF in December 1947 and January 1948 under lot 3217 at their St. Charles, Missouri plant. When delivered, these 31 seat parlor cars were named *Alton*, *Springfield* (here seen in St. Louis in September 1967), *Bloomington* and *St. Louis*. Note that these cars closely match coaches 3050-3060, shown on page 82. This is due to the fact that these cars were originally supposed to be part of an all coach order but were delivered as parlor cars instead. *(Paul Winters)*

Parlor 5931, series 5930-5931
▼ Another aluminum ACF built car from the eight car trainset built for the B&O in 1935, this parlor-drawing room car was found backing out of Chicago's Union Station in October 1967. It seated 24 in the parlor area and another five in the drawing room. Like much of the GM&O's passenger equipment, this car would be retired in September 1969. *(Ron Plazzotta)*

Parlor 5932, series 5932-5933

▶ Closely identical to the aluminum parlor car shown opposite below, this car was constructed of Cor-Ten steel by ACF in 1935 for the Alton's ABRAHAM LINCOLN service. It was spotted in Chicago in May 1967.

(Ron Plazzotta)

Observation 3040-*Chicago*, series 3040-3041

▲ *Chicago* was one of two observation cars built by Pullman in 1924 for ALTON LIMITED service as the Chicago and Alton's 680. (Sister 681 was named *St. Louis*, then as GM&O 3041, *Mobile*.) By the time of this photograph, taken while *Chicago* backs through St. Louis on September 5, 1953, the rear platform had been enclosed and end door and diaphragm added for mid-train use. Observation *Chicago* had seating for 39 passengers and would remain on the roster until the mass retirement of passenger cars by the GM&O in September 1969.

(Lawson Hill, Boston Chapter, NRHS collection)

Observation 5998, series 5998

▼ On July 17, 1965, the observation car of the ABRAHAM LINCOLN works its way past a sea of Pennsy equipment into Chicago's Union Station. This was a parlor-observation car and was part of the eight car aluminum trainset built for ROYAL BLUE service by ACF in 1935. A nearly identical Cor-Ten steel car was also built and numbered 5999. Capacity was 18 in the parlor and another 16 in the observation area. This observation would also be sent off to retirement in September 1969 although its namesake train, the ABRAHAM LINCOLN, would continue on into Amtrak. (Owen Leander)

Pullman Sleepers, *Judge Milton Brown* and *Culver White*
▲▼ These four section, one compartment, eight roomette, three double bedroom sleeping cars were part of a four car order placed with ACF in February 1949. They were delivered to the GM&O in July and August 1950 under lot 3208 from ACF's St. Charles plant (making for a rather rare introduction of ACF equipment into the Pullman sleeper pool). These cars were originally to have been named after famous generals but conflicts arose with existing Pullman names. The railroad then proposed to name the cars after cities on the route which also caused conflicts, and then states, which also conflicted with existing equipment. Eventually the road chose four names: *Judge Milton Brown*, *Culver White*, *Samuel King Tigrett* and *Timothy B. Blackstone*, which were adopted. *(Top)*, *Judge Milton Brown* (named for the president of the Mobile and Ohio during the Civil War) is seen moving through an interlocking (likely in Chicago) in May 1967. *(Bottom)*, *Culver White* (named for the then recently deceased Vice President of Finance) was spotted in Brighton Park, Chicago, showing the opposite side of one of these cars, on June 29, 1969.

(top, Ron Plazzotta; bottom, Owen Leander)

Business car 1
▲ Business car 1, shown here at some unknown location in March 1971, was originally built as a wooden car for the Mobile and Ohio in 1898 by the Ohio Falls Car Company, one of the predecessor companies that made up ACF. Apparently, in 1948, to conform with the new fleet of passenger equipment ordered around the same time, the railroad had ACF extensively rebuild this car with steel. Business car 1 (previously M&O's business car 2) was a general use car with no permanent assignment. *(Joseph Petric)*

Business car 50
▼ Business car 50 sits in Birmingham, Alabama on February 15, 1971 on the tail end of the Southern's train No. 2, the SOUTHERN CRESCENT. This car came from ACF in May 1928 under lot 474, built at Jeffersonville, Indiana, for the Gulf, Mobile and Northern as an all steel car. It was originally used by President Isaac B. Tigrett, then upon his death in 1953, by President Hicks until his death in 1958. It was then assigned to President Glen Brock until his retirement from the ICG in 1975. *(J.W. Swanberg)*

GM&O BOX CAR

Insulated Box Car 1244, series 1200-1247
▲ Our first Gulf, Mobile and Ohio freight car is this insulated box car built by General American in July 1963. Built under lot 8320, this group of cars featured ten foot Youngstown plug doors, Keystone 20 inch cushioning systems and Barber S-2-C trucks. UNARCO brand two piece load dividers and four position sidewall fillers were also installed into the fiberglass insulated interior. This 70 ton capacity, 4,360 cu.ft. rated car was photographed at some unrecorded location in March 1965. *(Emery Gulash)*

Insulated Box Car 1332, series 1330-1332
▼ The Gulf, Mobile and Ohio only owned a single series of outside post box cars and this was it. Built by North American Car it its Chicago Ridge plant in October 1965 under lot D-65-A, these cars had 20 inch Keystone cushioning systems installed, along with twelve foot Youngstown plug doors (a rarity for this North American car design) and twin Evans one piece bulkheads. Single position sidewall fillers were also used. Outside, Equipco model 3750E handbrakes and Barber S-2-C trucks were fitted. These cars were rated at 70 ton capacity and 4,565 cu.ft. This example was located in Canal Yard in New Orleans, Louisiana in April 1972. *(Jim Selzer)*

Box Car 6001, series 6000-6009
▶ This aluminum box car originated as the Alton's 1200-1209 series built by Mt. Vernon in June 1945. These were express cars with this one being assigned to Chicago-St. Louis service. These rather unusual cars were rated at 50 ton capacity or 3,898 cu.ft. That little logo panel in the upper left corner of the car is a special panel denoting the use of Reynold's Metals aluminum in the construction of the car which was quite unusual at the time of manufacture. Although this car was in stores service service (thus the 6000 series numbering) when spotted at Glenn Yard in January 1975, I've chosen to place it here with the other box cars. *(Ken Donnelly collection)*

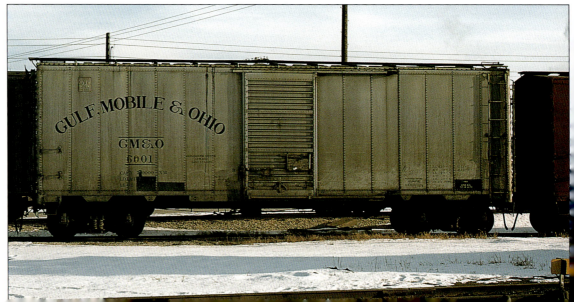

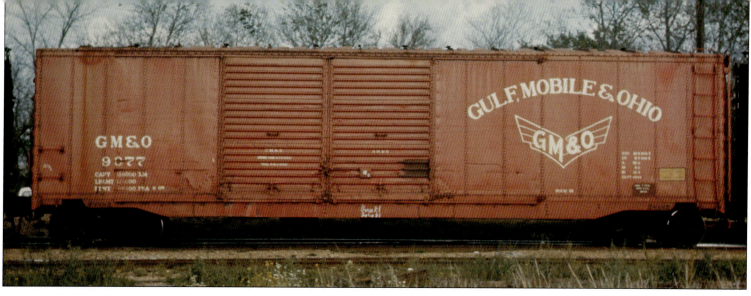

Box Car 9077, series 9000-9199
▲ Built by ACF in December 1950 under lot 3487, this winged herald car was found sitting in Canal Yard in New Orleans, Louisiana in April 1972. It was repainted by the GM&O's Frascati Shops in August 1968 from its original scheme which had "Gulf, Mobile & Ohio" spelled out straight across the cars' sides. These cars used ASF Ride Control trucks and Youngstown seven and eight foot sliding doors. Uncushioned, they were rated at 50 ton capacity or 4,844 cu.ft. *(Jim Selzer)*

Box Cars 9213 and 9562, series 9200-9599
▼▼ Two views of this series of cars is illustrated here so that early and late paint schemes may be shown. At *(center)*, GM&O 9213, built in December 1955, sits far from home in Reading, Pennsylvania on April 28, 1976. By the time of its repainting, the GM&O liked to use AAR car codes in addition to the normally seen mechanical designations, resulting in that "B202" nomenclature next to the regular "XML" stencilling. That "XML" designation inferred internal loader equipment though no information has surfaced to indicate what equipment was used. At *(bottom)*, box car 9562 is shown in as-built paint one month after its January 1956 manufacture while in Lawrence, Kansas. Built by ACF under lot 4565, this group of cars was rated at 50 ton capacity or 4,845 cu.ft. As an overall group, they were plainly equipped cars, lacking cushioning or exotic interior equipment. Barber S-2-C trucks were installed as were nine foot Youngstown doors. *(center, Craig Bossler; bottom, Don Ball collection)*

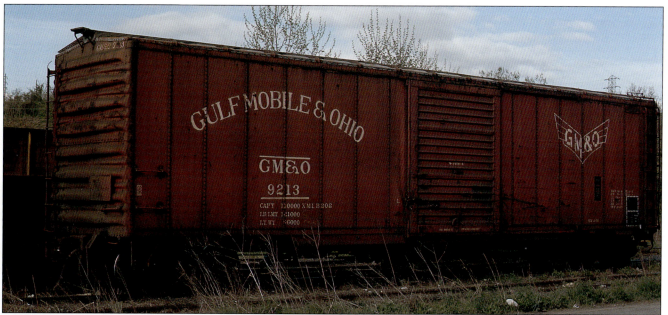

Box Cars 9657 and 9733, series 9600-9849

▲▼ Here are two views of cars from the same Pullman-Standard builders lot, 8380. At *(top)*, Huntsville, Alabama was the location where this car was seen in March 1970. Built by Pullman-Standard in December 1957, this PS-1 was equipped with a nine foot Superior door (likely a replacement for the original PS door), ASF Ride Control trucks and sported a "Do Not Hump" placard on the near tack board. At *(bottom)*, another car is shown with Pullman-Standard doors installed. This car was seen moving through Marion, Ohio, north of the Union Depot, in July 1962 while in an Erie Lackawanna westbound freight. These were plain cars, lacking cushioning or interior loader equipment and rated at 50 ton capacity or 4,840 cu.ft. It is interesting to note that while both cars have their factory paint, the black ends have turned almost brown due to the dirt and age on the upper car.

(top, Bernie Wooller; bottom Paul Winters)

Box Car 9902, series 9900-9949
▲ On June 2, 1971, the Southern Iron and Equipment Company of Atlanta, Georgia delivered the first of 50 rebuilt box cars for the GM&O under lot 1131. They had their side sills reinforced along with having their running boards removed and ten foot Youngstown doors installed. This made quite a change from their original ACF built appearance. These cars were rated at 50 ton or 3,900 cu.ft. Note the roller bearing conversion trucks under the cars. Here we see the cars just coming out of the paint shop at the Southern Iron plant in Atlanta.
(Southern Iron & Equipment Co. photo, Freight Cars Journal collection)

NIRX 15007, series 15000-15007
▼ In March 1962, the North American Car Company ordered eight insulated box cars from Pacific Car and Foundry for sublease to the Gulf, Mobile and Ohio. This car, built in August 1962, was rated at 70 ton capacity and 4,616 cu.ft. Because of the heavy insulation in these cars they had only a 50'1" inside length. As delivered from North American for the railroad's service, they came equipped with fork lift pallets, which were supposed to be considered part of the car, along with Evans bulkheads. These cars also utilized Hydra-Cushion underframes and ten foot plug doors. *(Conniff Railroadiana collection)*

Box Cars 21635 and 21984, series 21000-21999

▲▼ These two box cars illustrate the vast differences in paint schemes applied by the railroad's Frascati Shops in Mobile, Alabama. Both were originally built by ACF in June 1947 under lot 3057. GM&O 21635 *(top)* received her winged herald and arched lettering scheme at the shops in January 1967. When 21984 *(center)* went through those same shops in April 1966 however, all it received was the straight-lined spelling of the railroad name on the right hand side of the car. Also note the door differences: when originally built they were fitted with Superior doors, but 21635 has received a replacement Youngstown door. Since similar cars were also built by ACF as GM&O 22000-22419 (under lot 3141), which included Youngstown doors, perhaps this car's doors were taken as those cars were stricken. Box car 21635 was photographed at an unknown location in April 1976 while 12984 was at Huntsville, Alabama at an unknown date.

(top, Paul Winters; center, Bernie Wooller)

Box Car 24261, series 24200-24299

▶ The Gulf, Mobile and Ohio's Frascati Shops rebuilt this car in September 1970. It was originally built in December 1952 by ACF under lot 3663 as part of the GM&O's 26300-26999 series. With a ten foot Youngstown door and roller bearing conversion trucks, this car was found sitting in Huntsville, Alabama in February 1973. These cars were also fitted with Evans DF-2 loaders and lading band anchors as denoted by the symbology on the door. *(Bernie Wooller)*

Box Car 24584, series 24500-24589
▶ While not denoted on the car's side, this double door box car was rebuilt by the railroad's Frascati Shops in November 1967. They were apparently from the GM&O series 35300-35389 originally built by ACF in December 1947 and January 1948 as lot 3142. This car was rated at 3,899 cu.ft. and had twin seven foot Youngstown doors. Note the bulging end caused by shifting loads which were likely caused by failure to properly use the Evans DF-2 loaders and lading band anchors installed inside of the car. Its photo was taken in September 1971 at some unknown location. *(Paul Winters)*

Box Car 26468, series 26300-26999
▲ Repainted at the railroad's Frascati Shops in March 1968, this nice looking box car had apparently just been pulled out of the ditch when spotted at Jackson, Mississippi on January 12, 1970. Built by ACF under lot 3663 in December 1952, it was rated at 50 ton capacity or 3,899 cu.ft. and assigned back to the GM&O at Jackson, Tennessee for flour loading. Six foot Youngstown doors and Ajax handbrakes were installed and at least four cars from this series had roof hatches installed. A number of these cars were picked for several rebuilding projects over the years.
(Conniff Railroadiana collection)

Box Car 50116, series 50100-50124
▼ In November 1967, this car (along with the rest in this series) was picked from the 9000-9199 series (see page 89 for a car in that original series) for upgrading to AAR "XL" classification. With this upgrading came four Evans DF-2 belt rails and 90 lading band anchors. In addition, of course, the cars received that bright green paint. The ASF Ride Control trucks and Youngstown doors were kept. This car, assigned back to the railroad at Laurel, Mississippi, was spotted at some unknown location in February 1968.
(Paul Winters)

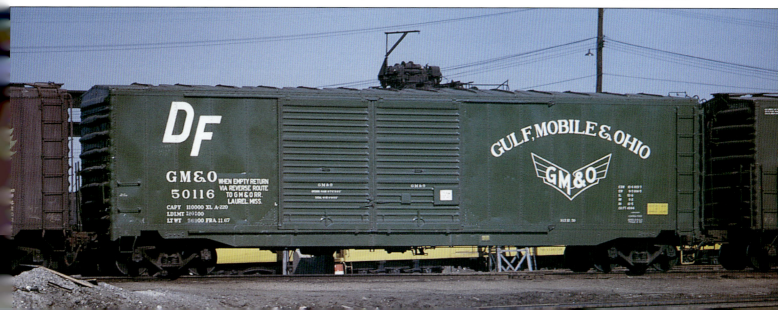

Box Car 52168, series 52000-52499

▲ These cars were originally built by Pullman-Standard under lot 5793 in April 1945 for the Alton. They would keep their Alton numbers after the takeover by the GM&O. This particular car had been repainted by the Gulf, Mobile and Ohio's Meridian, Mississippi shops on March 24, 1961. While the stencilling looks somewhat home made, note that the car still received black ends. A 50 ton capacity car rated at 3,901 cu.ft., it was caught sitting in the New York Central's McKinley Avenue yards in Columbus, Ohio in March 1963. *(Paul Winters)*

Box Car 53002, series 52500-53099

▼ Another ex Alton car is this brightly painted car found sitting in the snow at Fremont, Nebraska on January 25, 1969. It was rated at 3,899 cu.ft. or 50 ton capacity. Originally built by ACF in July 1945 under lot 2751, these cars also kept their original Alton number series after the GM&O takeover. Some cars from this series were picked for major rebuilding with ten foot doors in 1965 and placed into the GM&O's 24000-24099 series. *(Lou Schmitz)*

Box Car 54226, series 54100-54299

▶ A beautiful shot illustrates the lines of this Pullman-Standard PS-1 built under lot 8636 in September 1961. Taken north of the Marion, Ohio Union Station in July 1962, this car was in a westbound Erie Lackawanna train. This series of cars used either Barber or ASF trucks and all cars had seven plus eight foot Pullman design doors. Four DF-2 belt rails were fitted, though it is unknown whether or not these came from manufacture. This was a 50 ton capacity car rated at 4,940 cu.ft. *(Paul Winters)*

Box Car 55124, series 55000-55299
▶ Pullman-Standard furnished this uncushioned PS-1 to the GM&O in February 1970 as part of lot 9432. Found at San Luis Obispo, California on July 16, 1980 (having never been reweighed in the intervening ten years!) it was equipped with ten foot new design Pullman doors, Ajax handbrake and ASF Ride Control trucks. Inside, four Evans DF-2 belt rails were fitted along with Azee brand lading tie anchors. This was a 70 ton capacity car rated at 4,952 cu.ft. *(Peter Arnold)*

Box Car 56635, series 56500-56699
▲ Just leaving its Bessemer, Alabama birth place in February 1969, this PS-1 was part of an order to Pullman-Standard under lot 9374. These cars were equipped with four Evans DF-2 belt rails and door bars. Uncushioned, they rode over ASF Ride Control trucks. Cars 56500-56599 received Youngstown doors while 56600-56699 had the new Pullman design, as shown here. They were 70 ton capacity cars rated at 4,592 cu.ft. and (these two anyway) were assigned back to the GM&O at Montgomery, Alabama when empty. *(Pullman-Standard photo, Freight Cars Journal collection)*

Box Car 57591, series 57500-57799
▼ Proudly proclaiming the fact that it had cushioning (a Pullman-Standard Hydroframe-40 installation) this car sits in the yard at East Hazelcrest, Illinois on June 13, 1982. Built by Pullman-Standard under lot 9187 in February 1967, it was assigned to the GM&O at Tuscaloosa, Alabama when empty. Besides the 20 inch cushioning system, a Universal model 7400 handbrake was installed along with ten foot Youngstown doors. Inside, this 70 ton capacity, 4,932 cu.ft. car featured four Evans DF-2 belt rails and door bars. Either Barber S-2-C or ASF Ride Control trucks could be found in this order. *(Ray Kucaba)*

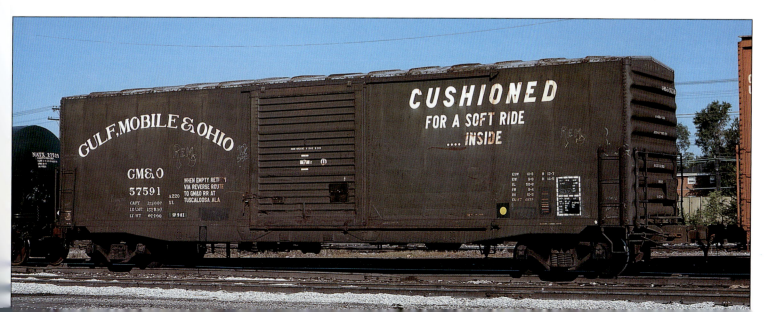

Box Car 57850, series 57800-57999
▲ Built by General American under Office Order 8399 in April 1968, this car was in assigned service back to the road at Jackson, Mississippi when it was photographed in September 1974, probably in Columbus, Ohio. These cars featured Barber S-2-C trucks, Keystone 20 inch cushioning systems and Youngstown ten foot doors. In addition, four DF-2 belt rails and an Equipco model 10024 handbrake was installed in each car. They were 70 ton capacity cars rated at 4,960 cu.ft. *(Paul Winters)*

Box Cars 58103 and 58136, series 58000-58199
▲▼ While both of these box cars were built by Pullman-Standard under lot 9315 in mid 1968, we wanted to illustrate several minor but distinctly different paint scheme variations. When spotted in October 1974 box car 58103 *(top)* had a large "DF" painted on its flank, added sometime after delivery. Compare to box 58136 *(bottom)* (assigned back to the railroad at Evanston, Mississippi) which still had its factory paint scheme when seen in June 1974. Both cars used Pullman's Hydroframe-40 cushioning system and ten foot doors along with ASF trucks and four Evans DF-2 belt rails inside. They were 70 ton capacity cars rated at 4,952 cu.ft. *(both, Bernie Wooller)*

Box Car 59102, series 59100-59103
▲ The Gulf, Mobile and Ohio only owned six 60' box cars, four of which are represented in this view. Built by Evans Products at their Plymouth, Michigan plant under lot 1-1009, this car sits outside the plant on a cold day in February 1967, the month that it was built. Built for auto parts service (in this case, assigned to the Rock Island at Ottawa, Illinois for auto glass loading) these cars used twin eight foot Superior doors and Barber S-2-C trucks. As was common with many auto parts cars, large numbers of belt rails (in this case 19 Evans DF-1 rails) were installed. Hydra-Cushion 20 inch cushioning systems were also fitted into these 100 ton capacity, 5,880 cu.ft. cars. *(Evans Products photo, Freight Cars Journal collection)*

Box Car 59270, series 59200-59299
▼ Shining in its brilliant green paint, GM&O 59270 was spotted in Joliet, Illinois in January 1964. Built in October 1962 by Pullman-Standard under lot 8745, it was assigned to the GM&O at Corinth, Mississippi when empty. This series of cars utilized Barber S-2-C trucks and Pullman's ten foot doors and Hydroframe-60 cushioning, a 30 inch system. Inside there were four Evans DF-2 belt rails and Azee brand lading band anchors. These cars were rated at 70 ton or 4,932 cu.ft. *(Emery Gulash)*

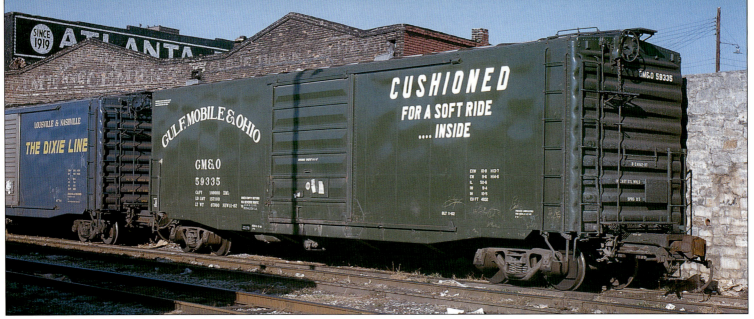

Box Cars 59335 & 59420, series 59300-59499

▲▼ As can be seen in the pages of this Color Guide, the Gulf, Mobile and Ohio returned to Pullman-Standard numerous times to place orders for 50' PS-1 box cars. One of these orders, built under Pullman's lot 8752, resulted in these cars built in November 1962. They were Hydroframe-60 cushioned cars equipped with ten foot Pullman design doors. Like most of the other green PS-1's ordered by the GM&O, this group of cars was fitted with four Evans DF-2 belt rails. Azee brand lading band anchors were also installed into these 70 ton capacity, 4,932 cu.ft. cars. Either Barber S-2-C or ASF Ride Control trucks were installed. These examples were both assigned to the GM&O at Bogalusa, Louisiana. Note that box car 59335 *(top)* found in Atlanta, Georgia in December 1963 was marked as AAR car class "XML" while 59420 *(center)* found east of 3rd Street in Columbus, Ohio in January 1963 was marked "XME." *(top, Howard Robins; center, Paul Winters)*

Box Car 59684, series 59500-59699

◀ Another Pullman-Standard PS-1 is this car manufactured in September 1963 under lot 8835. Assigned back to the railroad at Bogalusa, Louisiana, this car used nine foot Pullman design doors and had a Pullman Hydroframe-60 cushioning system installed. These cars also used four Evans DF-2 belt rails and interior lading band anchors and were rated at 70 ton capacity or 4,932 cu.ft. Within this order, 50 cars used Barber S-2-C trucks while the remainder received ASF's version.

(Paul Winters)

Box Car 103045, series 103000-103149

▶ In the 1950's, Evans and General American went into partnership together which resulted in a number of cars being constructed by General American with Evans furnishing the interior equipment. Many of these cars were then leased to various railroads including the Gulf, Mobile and Ohio. One of these cars was spotted at Jackson, Mississippi at an unknown date. Assigned back to Bogalusa, Louisiana when empty, it was leased by the railroad in 1960 and had eight DF-1 belt rails and doorway bars, numerous DF-1 crossmembers and ten deckboards and bulkheads. Built in November 1950 and equipped with an eight foot Youngstown door this 50 ton capacity car was rated at 4,872 cu.ft.

(Art Richardson)

Box Cars 440050 and 440081, series 440000-440099

▲▼ I just couldn't resist showing two photos of this series of cars. One has bright red paint and the other with more faded paint but from an excellent overhead vantage point, a view not often seen in print. Both cars are rebuilds from Southern Iron and Equipment out of their Atlanta, Georgia plant under lot 1154. Rebuilt from the GM&O 26300-26999 series (with the first car delivered on January 12, 1972) these cars received lower sill reinforcement channels and larger ten foot Youngstown doors. They were rated at 55 ton capacity, had ASF trucks and a capacity of 3,898 cu.ft. At *(center)* 440050 is shown as it appeared in St. Paul, Minnesota on a cold February 12, 1978 while *(bottom)* 440081 sits in the sunshine at Council Bluffs, Iowa on May 4, 1974. *(center, Ray Kucaba; bottom, Lou Schmitz)*

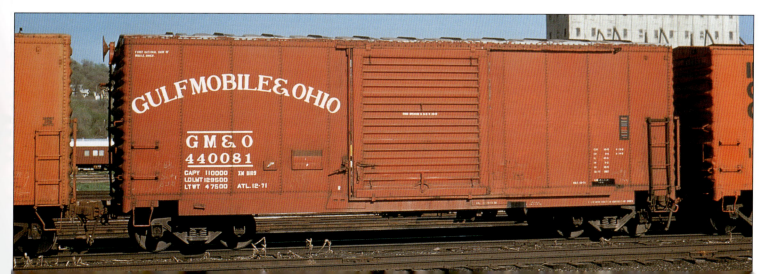

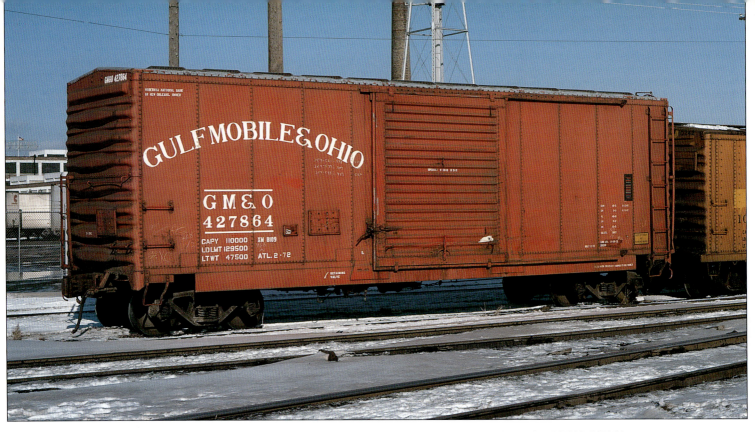

Box Car 427864, series 427750-427899

▲ Like the two cars on the prior page this box car also was a Southern Iron and Equipment rebuild from their Atlanta, Georgia shops. They were rebuilt in late 1971 and early 1972 and also originated from the GM&O 26300-26999 series (built by ACF in 1952 and 1953). SIECO's lot number was apparently 1142, with these cars originally intended to be delivered as GM&O 9850-9899, but this order was likely changed with this series the result. Large lower sill reinforcement channels and the ten foot Youngstown doors are the give aways to the rebuilding of these 3,898 cu.ft. capacity cars. This example was spotted in the snow at Bedford Park, Illinois on February 8, 1976. *(Ray Kucaba)*

Box Car 567001, series 567000-567044

▼ A highly unusual rebuilding was this group of cars rebuilt by Southern Iron and Equipment in May 1972 under lot 1164. With an obvious move toward strengthening the ends, the rebuilding entailed complete replacement of the ends with flat plate and heavy duty beams. In addition, they used a rather unusual nine foot plus six foot Youngstown door arrangement, further completing the strangeness of the car design. These were 55 ton capacity cars rated at 4,758 cu.ft. Assigned to the railroad at Laurel, Mississippi, one of these exotic creatures was found in Huntsville, Alabama in November 1973.

(Bernie Wooller)

HOPPER GM&O

Open Hopper 60173, series 60000-60749
▲ In March 1944, ACF built 750 war emergency composite twin hoppers under lot 2637 for the Alton. (Additional cars had also previously been constructed by General American in November 1943 and placed in the Alton's 60750-60849 number series.) In late 1955 or early 1956, one car from this series plus one from the General American built series were converted to all steel, possibly as a trial run. By late 1959, all cars from both series had been converted to all steel. The rebuilding consisted of all new sides, as this view taken at Coxton, Pennsylvania in June 1966, shows. *(Dr. Art Peterson)*

Open Hopper 61505, series 61500-61549
▼ This string of Pullman-Standard PS-3 open hoppers was photographed by the company photographer just after their repainting at Jackson, Tennessee in December 1965, where it is believed the photo was taken. These cars had been originally built in October 1957 for the DT&I (as that road's 1700-1749 series) and acquired second hand by the GM&O for rebuilding to wood chip hoppers. This rebuilding, which occurred at Frascati in 1966 and 1967, consisted of the addition of four foot, ten inch side and end extensions. After the modifications they were renumbered to GM&O 82400-82449. *(GM&O photo, Ken Donnelly collection)*

Open Hopper 62164, series 62000-62299
▲ This triple open hopper was found sitting in Melrose Park, Illinois on January 14, 1980 with a load of coal. Considering the fact that it was built in January 1954 (by Pullman-Standard under lot 8076) for ore service, it is nothing short of amazing that it is in such good shape. These 100 ton capacity, 1,629 cu.ft. cars used Miner model D-3290 handbrakes and either Barber S-2-A or ASF Ride Control trucks. (Looking closely, one can see that these trucks have enclosed bearings.) Door locks were Monoloc brand. *(Ray Kucaba)*

Wood Chip Hopper 82272, series 82200-82343
▼ Another interesting hopper is this 50 ton capacity, 3,500 cu.ft. wood chip hopper. Rebuilt by the railroad's Bloomington, Illinois shops in 1962 from the GM&O series 61000-61149 (built by ACF for the Alton in April 1945 under lot 2752) these cars were quite tall with an overall height of almost twelve feet, one inch. Note the car shaker bracket installed near the middle of the car to assist in clearing the car's load. This car was spotted in the midday sun at Mobile, Alabama on September 5, 1983. *(Dave Wagner)*

Wood Chip Hopper 82673, series 82550-82799

▶ The Gulf, Mobile and Ohio went to Greenville Steel Car in 1967 and 1968 for these oversized wood chip cars. Built under Greenville's Office Order 920 in May 1967, this faded example was spotted in Meridian, Mississippi under load on March 14, 1984. These were huge cars at 15' overall height and 56'1" inside length. While only rated at 70 ton capacity, they could carry 5,748 cu.ft. of chips. Barber S-2-A trucks were fitted as were Wine door locks. Though hard to see in this lighting, close examination would reveal the small waffles pressed into the car's side sheets to help stiffen up the sides.
(Ray Kucaba)

Wood Chip Hopper 866342, series 866300-866399

◀ When the Gulf, Mobile and Ohio received these additional (to GM&O 82550-82799, illustrated above) wood chip cars from Greenville Steel Car in 1972 under Office Order 1043, they received six digit numbers to better fit into the new overall numbering plan for the upcoming postmerger ICG system. Built in March 1972, 866342 sits under load at Meridian, Mississippi on March 14, 1984. Equipped with Barber S-2-A trucks, an Equipco model 4000-A handbrake and Wine door locks, this car was rated at 70 ton capacity or 5,748 cu.ft.
(Ray Kucaba)

COVERED HOPPER GM&O

Covered Hopper 80007, series 80000-80049

▶ This 70 ton capacity, 1,958 cu.ft. covered hopper was spotted in Tuscaloosa, Alabama on October 4, 1980. It was built by Pullman-Standard in 1946 under lot 5851 (note that the car is incorrectly stencilled as having been built in March 1953). Assigned to the railroad at Mobile, Alabama, it had ASF Ride Control trucks and Ajax handbrake installed. Standard Railway Equipment Company three foot by three foot square hatches were also installed as were Enterprise outlets. *(Ray Kucaba)*

Covered Hopper 80507, series 80500-80549

▶ In 1949, ACF built fifty 70 ton, 1,958 cu.ft. capacity covered hoppers for the GM&O under lot 3302. These plain cars utilized Barber S-2-A trucks and Enterprise outlets. Still carrying remarkably clean paint, covered hopper 80507 was hard at work when spotted in Crestline, Ohio in October 1980 in an eastbound Conrail train.
(Larry DeYoung)

Covered Hopper 80712, series 80700-80749

▲ In November 1962, Pullman-Standard manufactured this car under lot 8753. Built to a 70 ton, 3,219 cu.ft. PS-2 design it sits in Tuscaloosa, Alabama on March 14, 1984. These cars rode on Barber S-2-A trucks and had ten 30 inch round hatches per car. Underneath were Enterprise outlets. *(Ray Kucaba)*

Covered Hopper 80957, series 80900-80974

▼ Another product of Pullman-Standard was this 70 ton capacity, 3,215 cu.ft. PS-2. Built in August 1961 under lot 8588, it was similar to the car above but rode on ASF Ride Control trucks. It was found sitting in Paducah, Kentucky on September 27, 1991. *(Ray Kucaba)*

Center Flow 81016, series 81000-81049

▲ The Gulf, Mobile and Ohio only owned one series of ACF Center Flow covered hoppers. They were built under lot 11-02392 in May 1966. Cars from this order are shown during the delivery process, presumably at ACF's plant. They were 100 ton capacity cars rated at 4,600 cu.ft. apiece and were equipped with Barber S-2-A trucks and Ajax handbrakes. Six individual 30 inch diameter hatches were aligned down the car's top centerline and outlets were a gravity Keystone design. The cars in this photo were assigned to the GM&O at Fox, Alabama.

(GM&O photo, Ken Donnelly collection)

Covered Hopper 81084, series 81050-81149

▼ In August 1970, the railroad received 100 PS-2CD covered hoppers from Pullman-Standard's Butler, Pennsylvania plant built under lot 9431. These 4,740 cu.ft., 100 ton capacity cars were somewhat rare in that they used six centerline 30 inch diameter hatches in lieu of the much more common trough hatches normally found on 4,740 cu.ft. PS-2 cars. One of these car is shown here sitting in East St. Louis, Illinois on October 23, 1979. In addition to the roof hatches, Barber S-2-C trucks and Klasing handbrakes were fitted to this order. *(Ray Kucaba)*

Airslide Covered Hoppers 85001 and 85015, series 85000-85017

◄ From the first series of dual bay General American Airslide covered hoppers, these two cars illustrate the subtly different paint schemes that these cars featured. At *(top)*, 85001 is shown sitting in Cedar Rapids, Iowa on a snowbound March 6, 1984. At *(center)*, 85015 sits in Allentown, Pennsylvania on March 31, 1972. While both cars have the General American logo in the upper left corner of the car, notice how the reporting marks and car number styles differ greatly along with the fact that 85001 is missing the lines above and below this information. Both cars were built by General American in July 1964 under Build Order 8359-O. They were rated at 100 ton capacity or 4,180 cu.ft. and used Barber S-2-A trucks. While it is easy to note that the return stencilling on 85015 is back to the MP agent in Atchison, Kansas, 85001's routing is much harder to see: it is for the return of the car to the Rock Island at Enid, Oklahoma, a long way from home rails.

(top, Ray Kucaba; center, Craig Bossler)

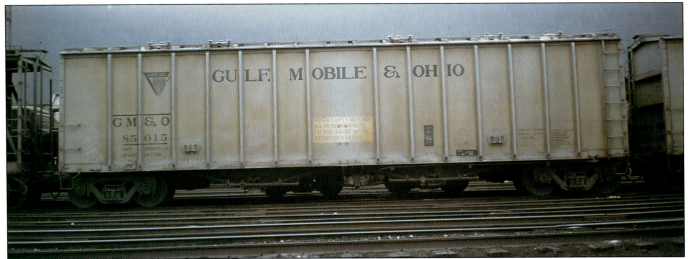

Airslide Covered Hopper 85025, series 85018-85035

▼ In February 1966, the GM&O returned to General American for more dual bay Airslide covered hoppers. This group of cars was built under Build Order 8376-G. One of these cars is shown far from home at San Luis Obispo, California in July 1981. Although dirty, note that this cars' reporting mark and number style differs slightly from either of the cars shown above. Modelling all three variants and placing them on one train would be a neat eye opener! These cars were very similar to the ones received in 1964 and were also 100 ton capacity, 4,180 cu.ft. cars. General American also provided additional cars in the GM&O series 85036-85045 built under Build Orders 8385-E and 8395-C in mid to late 1967. *(Peter Arnold)*

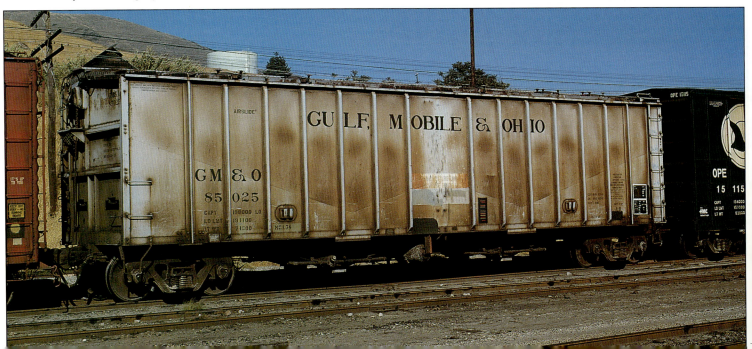

Leased Airslides 44364 and 44368, series GACX 44361-44382
▲▼ These two cars are part of a small group of Airslide cars that General American leased to the Gulf, Mobile and Ohio. The car at *(top)* was in sugar service when spotted in St. Paul, Minnesota on February 12, 1978. It was built by General American in June 1960. Careful observation will reveal that those 20 inch round hatches have gasket material showing from under the hatch covers, a feature not often seen from trackside, (and proving the value of overhead photos) nor often modelled. The photograph at *(bottom)* shows covered hopper 44368 at its home base in Springfield, Illinois on June 26, 1984. This car was built one month later than the car illustrated above, in July 1960. Both of these cars were 2,600 cu.ft. cars rated at 70 ton capacity. Additional cars of this design also known to be leased to the GM&O were GACX 42402-42406 and 43438-43457. *(both, Ray Kucaba)*

GM&O FLAT CAR

Pulpwood Flat 3571, series 3500-3599
▲ The Gulf, Mobile and Ohio moved lots of pulpwood and required a number of varying cars to protect this traffic. This car was part of a series built by Thrall Car and Manufacturing under lot 325 in September 1966. Found in Vicksburg, Mississippi on September 29, 1991 pulpwood flat 3571's paint, while original, has gotten a bit ragged due to all the abuse it endured in this service. These 70 ton capacity cars used Barber S-2-A trucks and were an even 50' long between bulkheads. *(Ray Kucaba)*

Pulpwood Flat 3677, series 3600-3749
▼ Magor Car Company built this pulpwood car in May 1966 under their lot 15018. Like the car above, it was a 70 ton capacity car with an even 50' between bulkheads although the cars in this series used ASF Ride Control trucks. Pulpwood 3677 was also spotted in Vicksburg on September 29, 1991. *(Ray Kucaba)*

Pulpwood Flat 3894, series 3750-3999

▶ Pulpwood, a big source of low value traffic on the GM&O, required large quantities of pulpwood flats. In an effort to gain the needed cars at a price they could afford, the railroad helped General Steel Castings develop the cast pulpwood flat car. This cast car was intended to be provided to the railroads as "kits" which the road was to add trucks, brakes and paint to finish off. In 1957, the GM&O built this series of cast flats, using various secondhand trucks (and likely other parts) to further keep the cost down. Under load, one of these cars was still on the job on November 9, 1985 at Jackson, Mississippi. *(Ray Kucaba)*

Pulpwood Flat 4698, series 4600-4699

▲ Another cast flat is this car, built from a General Steel Castings cast flat kit at the railroad shops in April 1954. The road acquired some 1,150 cars of this design from 1950 through 1957. Like most of them, this car (found sitting in a Chicago, Illinois dead line on April 28, 1985) used second hand components. On this car, ASF Ride Control trucks were fitted. While the paint on this car is rough (like most pulpwood cars, heavy usage was the norm) the GSI cast-in logo is easily noted from the fortunate sun angle. *(Ray Kucaba)*

Pulpwood Flat 4911, series 4901-4926

▼ On March 25, 1969, the Southern Iron and Equipment Company of Atlanta, Georgia delivered the first of 25 pulpwood flats rebuilt from box cars to the GM&O under lot 853. The GM&O supplied box cars out of the 21000-21999 series, built by ACF in 1947, for this program. This example was found sitting in Mize, Mississippi on November 9, 1985. With an inside length of 35' 1/2", this 50 ton capacity car rode on ASF Ride Control trucks. *(Ray Kucaba)*

Bulkhead Flat 74093, series 74050-74099

▶ Not all General Steel Industries cast flats were pulpwood cars as this regular bulkhead flat shows. It was originally built by the railroad in November 1953 as part of the GM&O's 72050-72139 series of "kit built" regular 53'6" flat cars. In October 1959, the railroad's Meridian, Mississippi shops modified 50 cars for wallboard service by the addition of cast bulkheads. (General Steel's design easily allowed this option.) This bulkhead flat was caught on the move east of 4th Street in Columbus, Ohio in August 1962. It is in assigned service back to the railroad at Mobile, Alabama and was a 50 ton capacity car with a 48'6" inside length between bulkheads.
(Paul Winters)

Bulkhead Flat Car 74582, series 74575-74589

▲ Thrall Car and Manufacturing built this bulkhead flat for the railroad in 1965 under lot 240 in July 1965. These all welded cars were rated at 70 ton capacity and had inside lengths of 49'6". ASF Ride Control trucks were included along with 36 lading strap anchors. Although normally assigned to wallboard service, when this car was spotted in Jackson, Mississippi on November 9, 1985 it was carrying large conduits. It was normally assigned back to the road at Laurel, Mississippi. *(Ray Kucaba)*

Bulkhead Flat Car 74726, series 74725-74759

▼ In May 1965, Thrall Car and Manufacturing built this car under lot 239. In addition, Thrall had previously built additional cars under lot 186 in September 1964 and placed them into the 74700-74724 number series. All cars were rated at 100 ton capacity and had internal lengths of 61 feet. This car, shown in lumber service at an unknown location in June 1965, was assigned back to the GM&O at Artesia, Mississippi. ASF Ride Control trucks with WAB-COPAC truck mounted brakes were installed. In addition, it was supposed to have 15 Brandon load binders, winches and chains fitted to help secure the load, though several appear to be missing. *(GM&O photo, Ken Donnelly collection)*

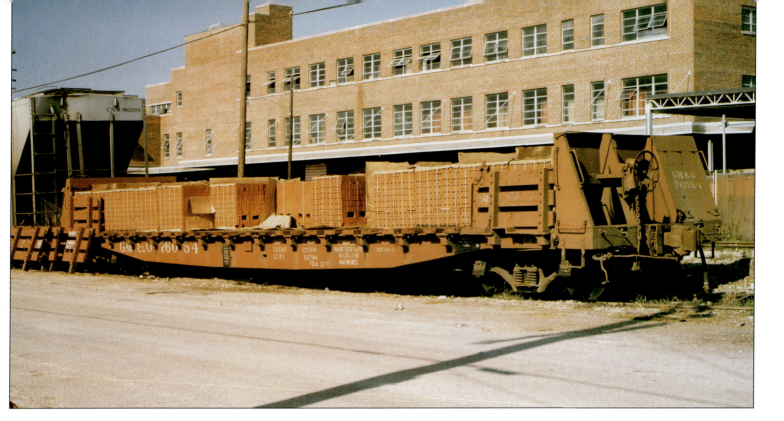

Bulkhead Flat Car 76054, series 76050-76055
▲ In December 1971, the GM&O's Frascati Shops converted this car for brick service. Apparently cars were converted from the original 72000-72049 series (built in 1951 by the railroad from General Steel Industries provided cast flats) more or less as needed, with the conversions occurring between early 1969 through late 1972. They were provided with four foot end bulkheads along with removable three foot high oak side panels to help contain the load of bricks. GM&O 76054, found in the process of being unloaded in New Orleans, Louisiana in November 1974, was assigned to the railroad at Macon, Mississippi. These cars were rated at 50 ton capacity and had between bulkhead lengths of 49' 3 1/2". *(Mike Palmieri)*

Refrigerator NRC 19578, series 19500-19749
▼ Leased to the Gulf, Mobile and Ohio, this Merchants Despatch Transportation owned refrigerator car sits in a Soo Line yard at Schiller Park, Illinois on May 2, 1975. Note that this cars last reweigh date is October 1959! This order of refrigerator cars was built by Pacific Car and Foundry in 1956 under lot 561. It is believed, though not confirmed, that all of the cars in this series were originally leased to the GM&O. *(Ray Kucaba)*

GM&O GONDOLA

Gondola 10106, series 10100-10124
▶ While this 65'6" mill gondola has certainly seen better days since it was built by Pressed Steel Car in 1948 (under lot 3415) it would be hard to find a better broadside photo showing the lines of these cars. Spotted in Matteson, Illinois in September 1980 it was still in service, likely hauling the steel products it was originally designed to carry. Note that there is a hand written "export-New Orleans" written on the car's side. While the railroad diagram sheet for this car specifies Barber S-2-A trucks for these cars, this car has a mixture of two truck designs under it. These cars originated as the series 10025-10049 but were renumbered when the railroad removed the drop ends and installed solid ones in mid 1965. *(Bob Simons)*

Gondola 13150, series 13150-13152
▲ In May 1967, the Frascati Shops converted three ex composite 41'6" inside length gondolas for shredded scrap metal service. Part of the modification entailed the addition of side and end extensions. In October 1974, one of these unusual cars was found on the Southern mainline at Birmingham, Alabama. These cars apparently derived from the Alton 44000-44249 series, built by General American in mid 1944. This car appears to have a build date of March 1944. *(Jim Thorington)*

Gondola 13239, series 13200-13251
▼ This car, built in May 1941, was acquired second hand from the United States Railway Company in 1968. It had previously been part of the DT&I series 7000-7299 built by Greenville Steel Car under Office Order 312. Rated at 50 ton capacity or 1,368 cu.ft., and with an inside length of 41'6", these cars had Ajax handbrakes (or at least they did prior to USRE's rebuilding) and wood floors installed. A variety of trucks were fitted. On August 12, 1987, this gondola was found sitting in Forest View, Illinois. *(Ray Kucaba)*

**Gondola 48015
series 48000-48019**

▶ While the paint is certainly raw on this 41'6" inside length gondola, I wanted to show that these smaller gondolas certainly were still active as late as September 22, 1978 when this car was found with a load of scrap metal in Harvey, Illinois. Built by ACF in October 1953 as lot 4120, these cars were originally assigned the GM&O number series 14400-14799. From 1952 on through 1962 they were converted to covered gondolas and renumbered to the series presented here. Not only does this car lack its roof but it was incorrectly stenciled "GRB" instead of the correct "GBR" required for a covered gondola. *(Ray Kucaba)*

INTERMODAL GM&O

Trailer RGMZ 204923, series 204917-204926

▲ In late 1964, Dorsey built ten 40' trailers for REA Leasing to be subleased to the GM&O. Registered in Minnesota, each trailer had a capacity of 2,442 cu.ft., and was 39' 6 3/8" long inside with an internal width of seven foot, nine inches and an even eight foot internal height. This photo is believed to have been taken at Dorsey's plant in 1964. *(Glyn L. Burke, Ken Donnelly collection)*

Autorack, KTTX 904284

▼ Another low deck rack car is this TTX class F89fh car carrying Ford Pintos. It employs a Whitehead and Kales Lo-Tri-Pak hinged end trilevel rack and was manufactured by Pullman-Standard under lot 9139-B in June 1966. This photo was taken at an unknown location in March 1975.

(Paul Winters)

Autorack TTBX 908677

▶ With a load of Ford pickups, this TTX class F89ch low deck car sits at an unrecorded location in August 1972. This car, built by Pullman-Standard in November 1968 under lot 9330-A, uses a Whitehead and Kales fixed bilevel rack.
(Paul Winters)

GM&O CABOOSE

Caboose 2609, series 2600-2639

▲ Beginning in December 1965 (and on through 1967) International Car began a major rebuilding of the GM&O's 2700-series caboose cars at their Kenton, Ohio plant. These were ex Alton cars, illustrated below. The resulting cars were hard to tell from purpose built International wide vision cars unless one took the time to look at the rivet patterns on the sides. As they went through the rebuilding process, they were renumbered, although not in order. Caboose 2609 (renumbered from 2732) was seen in Hattiesburg, Mississippi in September 1970 in company with GM&O gondola 10070. This gon, by the way, comes from the series 10050-10099 built by Bethlehem Steel in 1957 under lot 3400-268-F. These gondolas featured ASF Ride Control trucks and used "Tu Way" lading tie anchors. *(Howard Robins)*

Caboose 2711, series 2700-2739

▼ In 1946, the Alton Railroad received 40 caboose cars from ACF under lot 2883. They were numbered C-3025 to C-3064 by the Alton. When taken over by the GM&O in 1947, they were then renumbered into the GM&O series listed above. By the time of this photo, taken in Joliet, Illinois in January 1964, many (if not all) of these cars had lost their "A" end brake stands. That "NR" stencilled below the "radio" signified that this car was assigned to the Northern Region. With the major rebuilding by International Car (described above), this caboose was renumbered to GM&O 2618. *(Emery Gulash)*

Caboose 2741, series 2740-2744

▶ Prior to being absorbed by the GM&O, the Alton had been under the control of the B&O. During this period, numerous B&O cabooses were conveyed to the Alton and most made it to the GM&O. This ex B&O class I-5 caboose, shown here at Springfield, Illinois in March 1973, was originally built by the B&O at their Washington, Indiana shops in 1926. In March 1942, five of these cars (B&O numbers unknown) were transferred to the Alton becoming the Alton series 2802-2806. This car is ex Alton 2803. *(Walter Peters photo, Ken Donnelly collection)*

Caboose 2752, series 2745-2752

◀ When the B&O transferred 49 various B&O cabooses to the Alton on June 5, 1939, six I-1a cabooses were included, to be renumbered Alton C-2810 through C-2815. One of these I-1a cars (ex-Alton C-2815) is shown here in Chicago on December 26, 1964. Built by the B&O at Washington, Indiana in January 1923, it was originally B&O C-467.

(Owen Leander)

Caboose 2755, series 2755

▶ As one of the 49 cabooses transferred to the Alton from the B&O (on June 5, 1939) this I-5 class car was renumbered by the Alton to C-2818. It was built by the B&O at Washington, Indiana in August 1926 as B&O C-2029. Note that while this car is a class I-5 car (the same class as the car at the top of this page) it has kept its original sheathing while 2741 above has acquired plywood sheathing. Caboose 2755 was at an unknown location when photographed in November 1971. *(Ron Plazzotta)*

Caboose 2804, series 2800-2804

▶ The Alton acquired this caboose along with nine other ex B&O class I-1 cars on November 4, 1939. Built by the B&O (likely at their Washington, Indiana shops) in June 1916 as caboose C-268, it was apparently renumbered to Alton C-2875 after the transfer. On October 11, 1964, this caboose was found sitting in Chicago, Illinois. Note the home made uncoupling rod hanging from the rear railing! *(Owen Leander)*

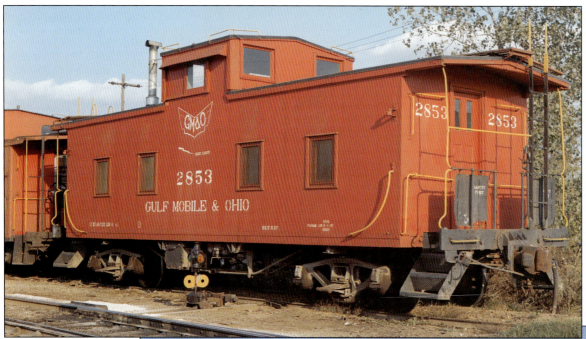

Caboose 2853, series 2847-2903

◀ This caboose, found sitting in Jackson, Mississippi on November 2, 1969, was once the Mobile and Ohio's X91. It was built in May 1927 and actually lasted until the merger with the Illinois Central. It is unknown at present if all of the cars listed above for this series are of this design although most are presumed so. Over the years, some cars in this group received plywood sides while at least one received steel sheathing.

(Art Richardson)

Transfer Caboose 2915, series 2909-2919

▶ In 1945, the Alton's Bloomington, Illinois shops took eleven flat cars from their 24000 series and converted them to transfer cabooses. Ten of these cabooses were then numbered as Alton C-3000 to C-3009 with the eleventh receiving the number C-3015. With its prior paint peeking through, caboose 2915 (ex-Alton C-3006) sits in Kansas City, Missouri, arch bar trucks and all, on May 3, 1970.

(Owen Leander)

Caboose 2955, series 2950-2958

▶ The GM&O purchased this series of wide vision cabooses from International Car Company in three separate orders. Cabooses 2950 and 2951 came in 1964 under lot 888, 2952 and 2953 were built in 1966 under lot 1023 while the remaining cars were constructed under lot 1320 in 1968. All of these cars came fitted with Barber swing motion trucks and Ajax handbrakes in addition to the Waugh ten inch cushioning system. This example was spotted at Springfield, Illinois on May 19, 1975. *(Roger Bee photo, Peter Arnold collection)*

Transfer Cabooses 2970 and 2977, series 2970-2985

▲▼ These two transfer cabooses were constructed from two sources. The cars' underframes originated with the GM&O box car series 5000-5683. The superstructures were manufactured new by International Car as kits which the railroad applied to the underframes at their Bloomington, Illinois shops in 1968. Caboose 2970 *(center)* was built upon box car 5152's underframe while 2977 *(bottom)* rode over 5119's. Friction bearing trucks were fitted as well as Equipco handbrakes. At least three different GM&O paint schemes were involved with these cars. Cars 2970 and 2971 received a spelled out road name and numbers. Cars 2972 and 2973 wore road initials and small numbers. The remaining cars, of which 2977 is an example, received initials and larger numbers. Both of these cabooses were spotted in Bloomington on September 27, 1975. *(both, Ray Kucaba)*

Caboose 2994, series 2989-2999
▲ This International Car built caboose sits in Jackson, Mississippi on February 14, 1971. These cars were built under two orders in 1970, 1671 and 1672. Apparently the difference was with the trucks; the first coming with friction bearing Barber swing motion trucks and the latter having roller bearing trucks. As the story goes, these cars were originally destined for the Erie Lackawanna but the EL was unable to finance these cars at delivery so the GM&O was able to acquire them, perhaps at a reduced price.
(Conniff Railroadiana collection)

Tank Cars 1805 and 1808, series 1800-1809
▼ These two interesting tank cars were spotted in St. Louis east of Compton Avenue in February 1963. Built by ACF in August 1957 under lot 02-5077, tank car 1808 is in original paint. Mate 1805 has been repainted by the road's Meridian Shops apparently in August 1962 (oil spillage makes the stencilling hard to read). These were 19,000 gallon, 70 ton capacity non insulated, non coiled ICC103W class cars. *(Paul Winters)*

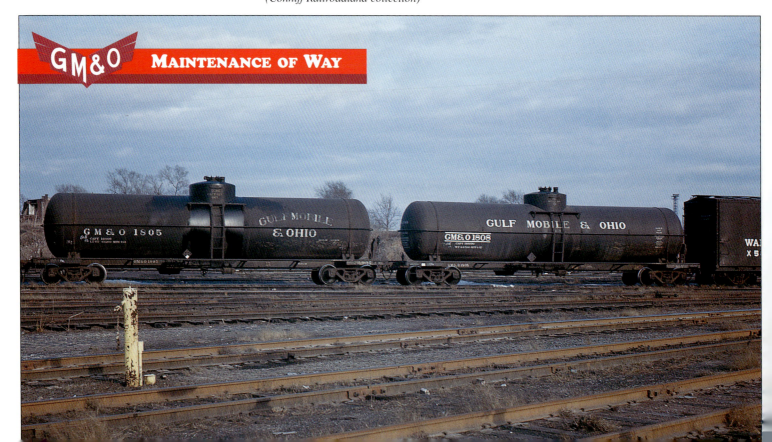

GM&O work equipment

▲▶▼ Here are three typical examples of the Gulf, Mobile and Ohio's work equipment. Like most work equipment cars little is known on their background and histories. For the modelers, these cars can present the ultimate challenge. At *(top)* is water car 66190, last repainted at Tuscaloosa, Alabama in July 1971. It was spotted at an unknown location in October 1972. At *(center)* is maintenance of way 67037, found on a wintry day after Christmas in 1964 at Chicago, Illinois. This car's history goes back to April 1925 when it was built for Pullman sleeper service under Pullman's lot 4763 and named *McCall*. It was later purchased by the railroad on January 19, 1949 and subsequently modified to coach 2204 on August 7, 1956. At (bottom) we see a 40' flat modified with low side boards for work service. It was found sitting in East St. Louis, Illinois on February 7, 1984 long after the merger. Information on the car's side indicates that it was last rebuilt in April 1965. It is a long way from its assigned home base of Montgomery, Alabama. *(top, John Furst; center, Owen Leander; bottom, Ray Kucaba)*

Jordan Spreader 66364

▶ This rare view shows a Gulf, Mobile and Ohio Jordan spreader (builder's number 1428) in action at Glenn Yard in Chicago, Illinois on June 6, 1972. I'm not too sure what the crew is trying to accomplish but it appears that they are trying to grade the access road. This unique piece of machinery would be scrapped at McComb, Mississippi in early 1997, keeping its GM&O reporting marks and number to the very end.
(Melvin Mowrer)

Work truck AD-21

▶ Although a bit blurred, this neat photo shows the photographer's F-500 panel truck at his home in Joliet, Illinois on a cold overcast January 12, 1961. Mr. Mowrer was the track supervisor for the line from Glenn Yard, Illinois to Bloomington, Illinois. As most GM&O work trucks were red, the blue may have been due to his high rank and ability to personally specify the color!
(Melvin Mowrer)

Work Truck AD-29

▼ Another GM&O work truck is this bridge and building Ford F-500 panel truck parked (under a no parking sign no less) in the yard at Mexico, Missouri in May 1970. That little dog house on the bed is the perfect touch to the truck. In the background is MofW 66924. This car is ex Mobile and Ohio baggage car 74, later GM&O 74. It was constructed by ACF in 1926 under lot 139 and was part of the M&O series 71-74. *(Bob Simons)*

On August 10, 1972, the Illinois Central and the Gulf, Mobile and Ohio merged resulting in a new paint scheme, primarily based on the existing IC's split rail scheme. On the following pages we present some sample cars illustrating the results of the merger.

Box Car 416224, series 416000-416951
▶ Our first post merger car is this stunning photo of an ex-Illinois Central 3000 series car found in Jersey City, New Jersey in February 1973. Built at the Centralia Shops in 1957, it had been repainted at that place only two months previously. This original series (also shown in IC colors on page 32) also supplied cars for several other renumbering projects for the ICG.
(Dr. Art Peterson)

Box Car 480069, series 480050-480069
▲ Built by Pullman-Standard for appliance service, one of these "mini" hi-cube PS-1's sits at San Luis Obispo, California on June 17, 1982. This car originated from the IC series 15450-15469 built under lot 9264 in October 1967 and was assigned to the Penn Central at Evansville, Indiana when empty. An additional ten cars were also built under lot 9264A and numbered 15470-15479, which went to ICG as 480070-480079. The first set of cars used seven DF-2 belt rails while the later cars used 13 DF-2 rails. These cars received Barber S-2-C trucks and Ajax handbrakes. Ten foot Pullman design doors and Hydroframe-40 systems finished these 50 ton capacity, 4,900 cu.ft. cars.
(Peter Arnold)

Box Car 545814, series 545800-545874
▼ Looking gorgeous in the afternoon sun in Long Island City, New York on September 29, 1976, this double door box car originated with the IC series 43050-43349 built at Centralia in 1962. These cars originally went to the ICG as ICG 545050-545349 but in 1975 the road rebuilt 75 at Centralia and placed them into this series. They kept their seven plus eight foot Youngstown doors and Universal model 1975 handbrakes but lost their running boards. This was a 70 ton capacity car rated at 4,971 cu.ft. *(Matt Herson)*

Box Car 580845, series 580600-580999
▲ The former Illinois Central's Centralia Shops kept their proud car building tradition alive after the merger with that facility manufacturing this car in October 1975. These were interesting cars with their waffled sides, Keystone 20 inch cushion underframe, Superior ten foot doors and Ellcon-National model D-16002 handbrakes. Barber S-2-C trucks were also installed. Inside, there were four DF-2 belt rails (placed within the waffle areas) and 108 individual lading band anchors in addition to continuous lading band anchors at the doorways. This box car was found in Bakersfield, California in April 1977. *(Peter Arnold collection)*

Box Car 590411, series 590300-590499
▼ This recently painted (April 1977 at Centralia) ex IC car was found sitting in October 1977 at an unknown yard (although likely out west, given all the western road cars in view!). They were originally built by ACF in 1967 under lot 11-06139 and placed in the IC series 11300-1149. A nice photo of one of these cars in brand new paint can be seen on page 35. It must have been quite a day railfanning with the new ICG paint and those new SP hoppers behind!
(Peter Arnold collection)

Box Car 660229, series 660213-660232

▲ Berwick Forge and Fabricating built this car for the ICG in March 1973 under lot 179-1. It came equipped with ten foot Youngstown doors, Barber S-2-C trucks, a Keystone 20 inch cushion system and an Ellcon-National model 1600-2 handbrake. Inside there were 28 rub rails and a one piece Evans Dual-Air Pak bulkhead. These cars were rated at 70 ton capacity or 7,440 cu.ft. This car was likely in appliance service and was assigned to the Penn Central at Evansville, Indiana. *(George Melvin collection)*

Container Gondola 220220, series 220220-220223

▼ Now here is a car that you just don't see every day! Converted to container service from a drop bottom gondola at Centralia in June 1974, this car was found in the midst of switching duties at Reading, Pennsylvania on October 17, 1976. While hard to see due to the slight blurring, note that the load limit is marked "with containers." The exact series of drop bottom gons that furnished this conversion is unknown at present although it is likely that they were picked at random from the IC's 99000-99743 series. These were 50 ton capacity cars rated at 1,956 cu.ft.

(Craig Bossler)

Gondola 245579, series 245550-245749

▶ A more conventional gondola is this Centralia built car found on the high iron at Belt Line Junction, Pennsylvania on May 7, 1978. Built that February, it was a 100 ton capacity car with an internal capacity of 2,000 cu.ft. These cars were intended for mill service. Note the oval cut outs in the side sheet near the floor line allowing interior load inspection from rail level. Barber S-2-C trucks were installed as was an Ajax model 15018 handbrake. Above each side post is a Tu-Way lading band anchor.

(Craig Bossler)

Coke Car 299904, series 299900-299904

▶ There is no way I was going to include a section on the Illinois Central Gulf without including this wonderful car! Apparently converted at Centralia in November 1973, it was under load when spotted in Tuscaloosa, Alabama in May 1974. The conversion obviously consisted of cutting off the roof, installing two sliding screen door openings on each end of the car and deleting the main door in lieu of a large screen door. These AAR class GDC coke cars were 50'6" inside length and rated at 4,864 cu.ft. or 55 ton capacity. Those little side doors measure six foot six inches wide by six foot eight inches high. While I don't know the previous history on these cars, that shouldn't stop anyone from trying to build a model of one of these cars! *(Jim Rogers)*

Open Hopper 320489, series 324000-324299

◀ Another interesting car is this ex Illinois Central hopper that had been rebuilt in May 1962 by the Centralia shops with a height extension of 14 inches. It had just been repainted at Centralia in February 1975 and caught on film later that month (on the 20th) while at Hazelcrest, Illinois. This extra height increased the cubical capacity to 2,540 cu.ft. on these 70 ton capacity cars. An Ajax model 14038 handbrake was installed as were Monoloc door locks. *(Ron Plazzotta)*

Woodchip Hopper 870000, series 870000-870199

▼ In what could easily pass for a builder's photo, class car 870000 sits in the yard at Fulton, Kentucky in April 1975, two months after its build date. Built by Pullman-Standard under lot 9779, these outsized cars were rated at 100 ton capacity or 7,000 cu.ft.; truly large cars. Barber S-2-C trucks were installed. As an interesting aside, the interior of these cars were lined with Ashland 510 paint, probably in an effort to ease the chip unloading.
(Ron Plazzotta)

Covered Hopper 765511, series 765300-765599

▲ In another photograph that could easily pass for a builder's view, this brand new Pullman-Standard 4,750 cu.ft. PS-2CD sits at an unknown location in the same month that it was built: September 1972. Built under lot 9605, these cars were equipped with Barber S-2-C trucks and Klasing model 1500-1 handbrakes. Keystone outlets were also installed as were four piece Apex brand fiberglass hatches. These may very well have been the very first Illinois Central Gulf cars to be delivered to the road after the merger, (not including ICG repaints). *(Paul Winters)*

Covered Hopper 766421, series 766300-766699

▼ By the time that these covered hoppers were delivered in March 1977, the lettering style had changed greatly from the first set of Pullman-Standard PS-2CD's delivered as shown above. Built under lot 9936, these 100 ton capacity, 4,750 cu.ft. cars were equipped with Barber S-2-C trucks. Either McLean-Fogg model D-8520-1 (766300-766499) or Ajax model 14665-1 (766500-766699) handbrakes were also utilized. The first 350 cars received Miner gravity outlets while the balance received a Miner gravity pneumatic design. All cars got a four piece fiberglass roof hatch. This car was found in North Platte, Nebraska on July 26, 1977. *(Peter Arnold collection)*

Flat Car 905057, series 905028-905299
▶ Working south of the border, this flat was seen moving really big logs in Nueva Casas Grandes, Mexico on March 20, 1975. It was originally built in January 1947 by the Illinois Central as part of the IC 60500-60999 series. These were 53'6" cars that were equipped with Barber S-2-A trucks.
(Matt Herson)

Flat Car 906112, series 906100-906164
▲ Another flat car with an interesting load is this car found at an unknown location in September 1984. This car was built by Bethlehem Steel Car in 1963 as part of the Illinois Central's 60300-60499 bulkhead equipped series. In November 1975 the ICG's ex GM&O Frascati Shops rebuilt them and deleted the bulkheads, reverting the cars to ordinary flat cars. Close examination of the ends of the car will show the remains of the old bulkhead installation. ASF Ride Control trucks along with an Ellcon-National model FA-158 handbrake were fitted to this car. Flat car fans should note the AAR approved blocking used for this load. *(Emery Gulash)*

Depressed Center Flat Car 940601, series 940601
▼ A one car series, ex GM&O 79000 sits empty in Harrisburg, Pennsylvania on September 6, 1976. It was built by the Gulf, Mobile and Ohio in March 1954 from a General Steel Industries cast flat. It was a heavy car (133,700 lbs. when last weighed at Centralia in May 1976). Note that there were two sets of brake equipment and accompanying Universal brand handbrakes. This 140 ton capacity car had a load carrying platform of 18 feet. *(Craig Bossler)*

Caboose 199062, series 199060-199064

▶ While you might not be able to tell, this caboose originated as a Western Maryland "Northeastern style" caboose. Acquired by the GM&O in 1964, they were quite heavily rebuilt by International Car in 1965. With the rebuilding, they received the GM&O numbers 2960-2964. These cars were commonly known as "Roodhouse" cabooses, probably due to their assignments near the terminal of Roodhouse, Illinois. This caboose, ex GM&O 2962, was found sitting in Chicago, Illinois in June 1975 having just left the Centralia paint shop one month earlier. As of this writing, this car still exists in private ownership at Manteno, Illinois. *(Bob Simons)*

Caboose 199102, series 199100-199116

▲ Another unusual caboose is this ex Pennsylvania N-8 cabin car. Found sitting in Council Bluffs, Iowa on June 3, 1980, this car was built by the Pennsy in 1951 and purchased in 1974. This series was originally numbered in the PRR series 23263-23282 and had Barber swing motion caboose trucks. According to the railroad diagram sheet, they still utilized their Duryea cushion underframes even after purchase by the ICG. *(Peter Arnold)*

Caboose 199399, series 199350-199449

▼ I just had to put this neat caboose in the volume! Built by the Centralia shops in 1972 as IC 9350-9399, one car was chosen for modifications for a research car. The result is illustrated in this view taken at Ft. Dodge, Iowa on February 23, 1982. Apparently it was used as a fuel monitor car at the time. Barber swing motion caboose trucks and Ajax model 14665 hand brakes were installed. *(Peter Arnold collection)*

Business Cars

▲ ▶ ▼ Just about everybody enjoys seeing a business car sail by, so we thought it appropriate to show some of the cars that the ICG used. At *(top)*, ICG business car 1 was photographed in Hazelcrest, Illinois in September 1973. It originated as the Illinois Central's number 1, shown on page 25. Note that the stainless steel railing motif has been changed to reflect the new corporate name "Illinois Central Gulf." At *(center)* business car 9 was in Chicago, Illinois on May 23, 1975. It also originated with the IC, as that road's business car 9, and is shown in IC colors on page 26. And at *(bottom)*, business car 10 was spotted at an unknown location in September 1973. This business car originated as the GM&O's business car 1, shown on page 87. It would be sold to the Louisiana Midland in 1974.

(top, Ron Plazzotta; center, Matt Herson collection; bottom, Ron Plazzotta)

The End